Sign of the Star

Sign of the Star

R. Earl Allen

BROADMAN PRESS
Nashville, Tennessee

for
my mother
my brothers
my sister
who shared our first Christmases

Preface

Christmas is an enchanted season! It is many things to many people, but it is much more to the Christian, because it is a wonderful reminder of the "good news." I believe strongly in the miracle of Christmas. It is the season when the human race pauses to be almost human again!

Christmas is songs and sentiment. It is moods, memories and, most of all, a message . . . of "peace on earth, good will toward men." No event in the history of mankind has had a deeper and more lasting effect than the Nativity.

Is it true that Christmas has become commercial, that we will have to choose Christ or Christmas? But there can be no Christmas for the Christian without Christ! Let us hearken back to "once upon a Christmas time" when Luke 2 said everything for us.

Phillips Brooks wrote, "O little town of Bethlehem, How still we see thee lie!" Oh, what emotions that "little town" has stirred in the hearts of people who have Christian faith. Blessed is that person who receives Christmas as a little child—with mysterious wonder. More blessed is that one who realizes it is a time of sharing not only our gifts but our faith. Really, Christmas is family, friends, and faith!

It is our hope that these devotionals will help you to experience a more meaningful Christmas. My deep appreciation to W. J. Fallis and William S. Cannon of Broadman Press and to Mrs. Alfred A. Brian, Jr. and Miss Arline Harris for their help with the manuscript. Also, an abiding gratitude must be expressed to those good, generous, and thoughtful friends of Floydada, Texas, who made it possible for us to see Bethlehem for ourselves.

Best wishes for a happy Christmas.

R. EARL ALLEN

CONTENTS

1
Portrait Painter

(Isaiah 7:14; 9:6–7; 53:1–12)

That God came to earth in the person of his Son is the greatest message of Christendom. What better time of renewal for our hearts than this season as we remember God's great gift to us? It is a time of light shining in the darkness—Jesus Christ, the Light of the world.

"The lamps are going out all over Europe," said Lord Grey, a British statesman in 1914, on the eve of World War I, "and we shall not see them lit again in our lifetime."

The darkness of sin entered the world in the disobedience of Adam and Eve; the light of righteousness faded away from the Garden. It was then that God first promised a Redeemer: Eve's seed would bruise the serpent's head.

Down the halls of history and the corridors of the centuries have rung the promises of God concerning Jesus Christ. Hebrews 1:1 tells us that God spoke "in time past unto the fathers by the prophets." In Genesis 49:10, we are told that the Messiah would be of the descendants of Judah. The prophet Micah pinpointed the place: "But thou, Bethlehem, . . . out of thee shall he come forth" (5:2). The prophet Daniel foretold the time of his birth

(9:25–26). Malachi described the forerunner of the Messiah (3:1). Jonah pictured in his experience the death and resurrection of Christ hundreds of years before the child was born in Bethlehem.

There has always been a desire in the hearts of men to know what Jesus looked like. None of the artists of the ages, try as they might, have ever achieved a completely satisfying portrait of Jesus. Many homes have pictures of him, but most of them reveal a lack of real knowledge of Jesus Christ.

The Gospel writers have given us eyewitness accounts of his life and work. But Isaiah, who lived seven hundred years before in some of the darkest days of the world's calendar, has, in a sense, painted the only really perfect picture of the Lord Jesus Christ.

Isaiah is sometimes called the fifth gospel, or "the gospel according to Isaiah," because he told us so much about what Jesus is like. It is a picture of deity mingled with humanity. Isaiah turned his inspired heart and mind heavenward: "The people that walked in darkness have seen a great light," he proclaimed.

Isaiah first described the immortal Immanuel. "Isaiah didn't really prophesy," Oswald Chambers wrote, "he was proclaiming—he was writing history aforetime." The words of Isaiah were prewritten history of God. "Therefore the Lord himself shall give you a sign; Behold, a virgin shall conceive, and bear a son, and shall call his name Immanuel" (7:14).

Jesus—"God with Us"

The great truth of Christmas is that God has come to dwell with us; the word Immanuel means "God with us." You can wrap up no greater Christmas gift. There is no Christmas present more important to your home. No greater bounty can be laid at the door of the poor. No Christmas remembrance to the brokenhearted is as comforting. No Christmas gift that comes to any soul is as important as the fact that God has come down to dwell among us. He was man's one complete need. He existed before the world was created. He lived before his birth in Bethlehem. He was active in the affairs of men long before Isaiah ever spoke of him. "Before Abraham was, I am," Jesus declared.

There is a section of England called Cornwall. A man who lived in a village there for a short time observed that it was an unusual place. "What makes this village so different?" he asked.

"John Wesley preached here a hundred years ago," he was told. "This village has never been the same since."

Jesus came to Bethlehem nearly two thousand years ago, and this world of ours has never been the same since.

"If Shakespeare were to enter the room," Charles Lamb wrote, "I would stand in respect to him, but if Jesus Christ came into this room I would kneel in adoration."

It is said that it took three thousand soldiers to keep the great Napoleon in exile. When he walked, the world of his day was shaken. His enemies knew there remained an underground of his following, so they assigned a small army to prevent him from regaining power.

But all the legions of Rome were not able to keep Jesus Christ in the grave. All the devils in hell are not able to separate Jesus from us. When God sent his own Son, wrapped him in swaddling clothes and laid him in the arms of a fleshly woman, God was identifying himself with us. Immanuel—God with us! Nothing shall ever take him away from us. Even the cross did not take him away except for three days. Then Jesus shed his graveclothes and came out of the tomb. It was not possible that the grave should hold him. Nothing could separate him from the people he came to live and die for.

Before he went away, he told his disciples, "It is expedient for you that I go away: . . . I will send [the Comforter, the Holy Spirit] unto you. And when he is come, he will reprove the world of sin. . . . He will guide you into all truth" (John 16:7–13).

His Wonderful Wisdom

Isaiah also pictured for us the wonderful wisdom of Jesus Christ. "Unto us a child is born; unto us a son is given"—he is ours! Isaiah went on to say, "And the government shall be upon his shoulder: and his name shall be called Wonderful, Counsellor, The mighty God, The everlasting Father, The Prince of Peace" (9:6).

In the Bible 256 titles are used for Jesus, trying to picture his majesty, his deity, his humanity—all the wonder of his abilities and attributes. Yet they are altogether inadequate. Perhaps the only time the word "wonderful" is used with complete accuracy is to describe him.

Isaiah could well have put a period after the word wondeful: "He shall be called Wonderful." Wonderful! What more can one say? Historians listed "seven wonders" of the ancient world. But there are more than seven wonders about Jesus. He was wonderful in his birth; he was wonderful in his life; he was wonderful in his teaching. He was wonderful in his death. He was wonderful in his resurrection; he was wonderful in his ascension. He is wonderful in his intercession; he is wonderful in his second coming. He is *altogether* wonderful!

Some of the best scholars say that the comma does not belong after "Wonderful." Isaiah declared that Jesus Christ is a "Wonderful Counsellor." All the other titles are double: mighty God, everlasting Father, Prince of peace. Elsewhere, Isaiah described him as "the Lord of hosts, . . . wonderful in counsel, and excellent in working" (28:29).

There are many kinds of earthly counselors. Quite often they have to say, if they are honest, "I don't know." But the counsel of Jesus is always perfect: "I am . . . the truth," he said. He had the answers. When people heard him speak, they said in awe: "Never man spake like this man" (John 7:46).

Until that time, Solomon had been considered the wisest man who ever lived, but Jesus said of himself, "Behold, a greater than Solomon is here" (Matt. 12:42).

But what is a counselor? He is a moderator, a reconciler.

It is said about Jesus "that God was in Christ reconciling the world unto himself" (2 Cor. 5:19). Jesus is the perfect counselor. He sat in the council chamber of God as an equal in the beginning, before the world was formed. He helped decide its creation and its redemption.

An earthly counselor should possess infallible knowledge. Jesus possessed *all* knowledge. He possessed undeviating rectitude, for he was entirely righteous and sinless. He had unlimited influence—"If ye shall ask anything in my name" (John 14:14). He had profound influence upon those with whom he was dealing, which was necessary, for you cannot help a man who does not respect you.

So wonderful was Jesus' knowledge that at the age of twelve, Temple classes were broken up so that the teachers of the Law could hear what this lad had to say. The wise men of the synagogue shook their heads; they could not account for his wisdom nor did they understand his mission.

Wonderful were his teachings, so wonderful that people hung on every word he said. Crowds followed him into the wilderness without thought of food; they didn't even take a sack lunch. So enthralling were his words that they refused to leave, wanting him to go on and on. The people were so satisfied with the bread of life he gave and the water of life he provided, that all they could think of was, "This is what we've been waiting for!" They did not think of food; they considered it a privilege to listen to him.

T. D. Talmadge said that he was sure some of the rabbis who had never preached to a crowd like that in all their years wagged their heads and criticized Jesus. "This foolish young man has nothing to say," they complained. "He is using unorthodox methods. He cares more about people than he does about the sabbath."

Wonderful were the words of Jesus, because he spoke with simplicity. The common people could understand him. He spoke the language of the streets—though not the language of the gutter.

Jesus spoke of the everyday things of life. He began one message, "If a grain of wheat fall into the ground and die." Another time he said, "A farmer went forth to sow." Jesus took familiar things as illustrations and applied them in teaching great truths.

Jesus counseled the brokenhearted. He said that for those who were sick there was balm in Gilead. For those who die, there will be a resurrection. To those who were sorrowful, he said, "Be of good cheer."

This great counselor held out his arms and said, "Come unto me, all ye that labour and are heavy laden, and I will give you rest" (Matt. 11:28). A long time before the psychiatrists of our day ever had their couches, the Great Physician had an altar. Peter advised, "Casting all your care upon him; for he careth for you" (1 Peter 5:7).

Prince of Peace

Isaiah called Jesus the Prince of peace. Some claim the title of "prince" by legend, by family ties, or by geographical boundaries. But Jesus promised, "Peace I leave with you, my peace I give unto you" (John 14:27). Isaiah said of him that "the government shall be upon his shoulder," for he is the only one fit to rule.

When Oliver Cromwell died, his brother assumed the right of an heir and set himself up as "protector of England." But it wasn't very long until Cromwell's brother laid down the responsibilities and went back to his farm. Government is a great burden to a man with a conscience; it is a heavy load to carry.

Jesus shall reign to the ends of the earth: "Of the increase of his government and peace there shall be no end" (Isa. 9:7). He shall be undisputed ruler; he shall be Prince of peace to all men. He is the King of kings. "He shall not fail nor be discouraged, till he have set judgment in the earth" (42:4). He will persevere until he has perfected his reign over all the earth and established justice.

Why is he our Prince of peace? He who is the author of peace is the only one capable of giving us peace. He has the right to rule because of what he has done for us. To any man who will give his heart to him, Jesus will give perfect peace in exchange. If we have his peace, then we must stand with Isaiah and say, "He *is* a wonderful counselor! He *is* the mighty God who can shake the earth! He *is* the Prince of peace!"

Already he is ruler in the hearts of men of every age and every race who love him.

When Billy Graham was ministering to the United Nations troops in Korea, on a Christmas Eve he and a chaplain found a young man dying on Heartbreak Ridge. The chaplain and Mr. Graham climbed up the slope and stooped over the soldier. The chaplain said softly, "May I help you, son?"

"No, it's all right," the young man answered.

The chaplain marveled at the soldier's tranquility in such an hour—until, glancing down, he noticed a New Testament clutched in his hand. A finger was inserted in the page where it is recorded that Jesus said, "My peace I give unto you" (John 14:27). They knew, then, the basis of the dying soldier's confidence.

When Jesus came, many of God's chosen people had almost given up. It seemed that God's promises would never be fulfilled. Israel had been broken asunder—ten tribes in one kingdom and two in the other. Then they were taken into captivity and dark oppression spread over their world for centuries. But Isaiah had said that the people who sat in darkness *shall* see a great light! The light came to them gradually. When you have been in darkness a long while, you can't stand much light at a time.

Then God began to unfold their books of prophecy. He brought the remnant of his people home. He sent angels to announce, "Here is your Messiah, your Redeemer, your Counselor who has come to save. Peace on earth, good will to men!" The governments of the earth shall fail, but never that of the Prince of peace. Greece will fail, Rome will lose its glory, but the kingdom of God shall prevail forever.

Suffering Saviour

Then Isaiah talks about the suffering Saviour. Near the cradle of Bethlehem stands the cross, God's Christmas tree—you can't make anything else out of it. The blood of Jesus Christ has been the red ribbon strung from that first coat of skins in the Garden of Eden down through the prophets of Israel, through the four hundred silent years, through the genealogies of the first chapter of Matthew. Crimson blossoms bright in the holy moments of the cross. That red ribbon wrapped around the cross—the blood of Jesus Christ—signifies God's gift to us. The cross is the most sacrificial gift of all, the one that required the most love.

Do not think Christmas can be bought with dollars and cents; Christmas bells are not the jingle of a cash register. Do not think Christmas can be found in the stores or in the warm glow of charity to the poor. Christmas points to the cross, the gift that only God could make. And it is a personal gift: "Unto *us* a child is born; unto *us* a son is given!"

Jesus suffered throughout his life. Joseph's profession was humble and one of the lowest paid. Poverty was the pattern of their lives, and the birth of Mary's firstborn son was evidence of their low estate.

His parentage was questioned in many ways. Mary suffered gossip and scorn. The Jews asked, "Can any good thing come out of Nazareth?" Jesus was a prophet without honor in his own country. When he performed miracles, the townspeople asked with knowing glances, "Isn't this the carpenter's son?"

The raging sea is calm compared to the sorrow that shook his soul. While Jesus walked the face of this earth he was despised and rejected. He was "wounded in the house of my friends" (Zech. 13:6). He has "trodden the winepress alone" (Isa. 63:3). A night is bright in comparison to the darkness he faced. He was bruised, spat upon, and humiliated.

More than you or I know how to suffer, Jesus suffered. The sun smote him. The cold chilled him. The rain pelted against his face. Thirst parched his throat. Hunger exhausted him. The cross killed him.

But God raised him up! For nothing "shall be able to separate us from the love of God, which is in Christ Jesus our Lord" (Rom. 8:39).

Do you want to know what Jesus looked like? You may find a picture in a store that will partially satisfy you. But only in Isaiah can you find a perfect portrait, that divine photograph the prophet glimpsed when the mysterious shutters of God clicked—seven hundred years before Christ was born.

Isaiah, you are right! Your picture is perfect. He *is wonderful!*

2
Faithful Forerunner

(Luke 1:1–25, 57–80)

One of the most impressive things about the Mormon Tabernacle in Salt Lake City is its wonderful acoustics. A pin dropped in the front can be heard in the back. In that receptive silence, just one pin makes what seems to be a tremendous noise. In the acoustics of God, the four hundred years between the Old Testament and the New Testament were full of silence. No warning prophet spoke, no inspired singer sang, no great deliverance was wrought by God. After Malachi, it seemed that the Word of God ceased. The heavens remained silent, the scrolls wrapped up, the voice of God unheard.

At last, a pin dropped. It was only the birth of a baby, a child who grew up to be a man of the wilderness, a new prophet through whom God spoke again. The writer who would tell the complete story of Jesus must start with this man called John the Baptist. He linked the Old Testament to the New Testament. John seemed like an Old Testament prophet transplanted into New Testament days, a prophet whose visions were fulfilled.

A Strange Birth

Strange things happened in relation to John's birth. Zacharias, his father, was a priest who served in the Temple at Jerusalem. As he ministered by the altar of God, Zacharias was visited by the angel Gabriel. The glory of the Lord stunned him as he listened to the great announcement of God that his childless home would be blessed with a son. Zacharias found the promise hard to accept, and he was struck dumb until after the event occurred.

On the eighth day after the child's birth, relatives and neighbors gathered. The father and mother had said nothing about a name. Those who were presenting the baby for circumcision concluded that he should be named Zacharias after his father.

His mother, Elizabeth, spoke up. "No," she said, "his name is to be called John."

Not willing to take a woman's word for it, the relatives thrust a writing instrument and tablet at Zacharias and asked, "What shall his name be?"

"His name is John," wrote Zacharias. Then his voice came back and he began shouting out loud for joy. All the people marveled. As the angel had said to Zacharias, "thou shalt have joy and gladness; and many shall rejoice at his birth" (Luke 1:14).

Under certain circumstances, Jesus declared, it would be better not to have been born. He addressed this particularly to those were stumbling blocks to little children. In these days we have sometimes heard people say, "I wish I had never been born." Or of some other, "It would have been better if he had never been born." Not so with John the Baptist.

There was a cheering section gathered outside at the birth of John the Baptist, not because the people knew what he would become, but because of the remarkable and long-awaited blessing coming to this godly couple. What joy—and what drama—the baby brought to that childless home!

One of the greatest things we can do in any day is to rejoice over a child and tell him that Jesus loves him. Or a youth, or an adult man or woman in the stresses of life. The greatest thing that can be said to any of us is the reminder that God still loves us. The only reason that people will rejoice over our birth is that we bring into the world something of hope, inspiration, gladness, and joy. Many people rejoiced at John's birth because John had a definite message to impart to the world, a word from God to give his generation.

Greatest Prophet of All

The Lord Jesus bestowed a special medal of honor upon his forerunner. He summed up the life of John: "Among those that are born of women there is not a greater prophet than John the Baptist" (Luke 7:28).

These two men present quite a contrast: John the Baptist and Jesus the Messiah. Their mothers were cousins. John was about six months older. Because of the closeness of the family, Mary saw a great deal of her cousin Elizabeth. It is likely that these two young men spent much of their boyhood together.

John the Baptist stepped into the mainstream of God's purpose when he appeared in the wilderness, "preaching the baptism of repentance for the remission of sins," and declaring that the kingdom of God was near at hand.

If we could keep only one memory of John, I would like to remember how he humbled himself before Jesus.

One day Jesus came and asked John to baptize him, as he had so many other people.

"Lord, I'm not worthy," John objected. "I have need to be baptized of thee, and comest thou to me?" (Matt. 3:14). John had declared to all who heard him, "There cometh one mightier than I after me, the latchet of whose shoes I am not worthy to stoop down and unloose" (Mark 1:7).

Later on, there came a time when Jesus took a towel and knelt in front of his disciples—Judas, Peter, James, John and the others—to wash their dusty feet. Simon Peter rebelled. "Master, you will never wash my feet! I'm not worthy!" But Peter was wrong, too.

When I was a young preacher, many times I accompanied Dr. W. A. Todd in summer revivals. Most of them were in little rural churches. Frequently Dr. Todd and I would share a bed out in the yard, on the porch, or wherever space was available for us—the best a humble home could offer. Dr. Todd was an early riser by habit. Often, when I awoke, I would reach under my bed for my shoes and find them freshly polished. What a humble gesture from a great teacher to his student! That godly teacher taught me more, perhaps, by shining my shoes than he taught me in the classroom.

Although John was close to Jesus, although there was blood relationship through their mothers, John revered and respected Jesus. He was not prejudiced because of familiarity as were the half brothers of the Master. It was revealed to John that Jesus was the virgin-born Son of God. When Jesus came to him, John said, "I am not worthy to baptize you." He felt he was not even worthy to tie the Master's shoelaces.

Look at a shoelace and let it remind you of the humility of this wilderness preacher. He was not blinded by the nearness of greatness in his life. This one that he had played with as a boy, he did not hesitate to recognize publicly as the one whom God had sent from heaven to earth.

The name God chose for the son of Zacharias and Elizabeth meant "gift of God." John was sent to be, as Isaiah had prophesied (40:3), "the voice of one crying in the wilderness, Prepare ye the way of the Lord, make his paths straight" (Luke 3:4).

Voice of Authority

Concerning John's preaching we would have to say that he was a very positive prophet. He heralded a proclamation from God, and he did it with great authority. Never do we find the law preached more plainly than by John. Never do we find love proclaimed more simply than by

Jesus. Yet there was perfect unity between them. One did not contradict the other; each complemented the other.

John presented a strange figure. He had taken the vow of a Nazarite. He did not cut his hair. His attire was very primitive. He "was clothed with camel's hair, and with a girdle of skin about his loins; and he did eat locusts and wild honey" (Mark 1:6). His nature-diet would cause a great deal of comment in our day.

Yet those who heard him preach soon forgot his strange appearance—they became conscious that God was there, speaking to them through John. It was not a dusky building, it was not a beautifully constructed, incense filled sanctuary. Yet somehow the Spirit of the Lord was vitally present in that sunny, arid wilderness.

John came to prepare the world for the Lord of glory. He spoke forthrightly of sin in the voice of a prophet, but he promised the coming of righteousness and peace. He thundered at the Pharisees and Sadducees, "O generation of vipers, who hath warned you to flee from the wrath to come?" (Matt. 3:7). He exhorted everyone, "Repent ye: for the kingdom of heaven is at hand" (3:2).

Popular Preacher

John the Baptist was also a popular preacher. Not that people listened because he was a polished man of pleasing words. But he did not behave strangely just for the sake of publicity. He had a positive simplicity in proclaiming God's message. His every word thrust home the doctrine of repentance. He declared the plain truth of God, asking no quarter and giving none. Do you know of any other preacher in history for whom the merchants have closed down their stores? Many in Jerusalem shut up their shops to go into the desert to hear John preach.

Today, people would advise him, "John, you need a better location to draw crowds. Come down to the city so that we can hear you."

In those days, the men of Jerusalem seemed to reason, "This man has words of life which are worth more than our merchandise. What he has to say is of more value than what we are doing. We will go out to the wilderness and hear him."

There John's listeners were not distracted by other voices. They were able to hear him plainly. He did not repeat what others had said. He had a fresh word from God for the people. He was a voice that proclaimed what God wanted him to say.

"Who are you?" people asked John. "Are you Elijah? Are you one of the other prophets?" He pointed them to "one mightier than I [that] cometh" (Luke 3:16). "Behold the Lamb of God, which taketh away the sin of the world" (John 1:29). John the Baptist said that he was only a voice for God.

Every man should know something of himself. John knew who and what he was. John was conscious that he was nothing but an instrument in the hand of God. Concerning Jesus, John declared, "He must increase, but I must decrease" (3:30). From the moment that the sons of

Mary and Elizabeth stood together in the waters of Jordan, that began to happen.

By the graves of some confederate soldiers whose names were not known when they were buried, this epitaph is written: "Who they were none knows; what they were all know." Who John was, John knew. He was not interested in making a name or a place for himself. He was interested only in cutting out the underbrush, making the road straight and smooth, preparing the highway of the Lord. John's single purpose was to get things ready for Jesus Christ.

That should be our aim, also. It is not ours to make a name for ourselves; it is ours only to proclaim the name of God, to preach the Lord Jesus. It is ours to clear out the underbrush, to do the slave's duty—and to do it whether anyone helps us or not. We who are called of God are committed to the task God sets us. Through our voices, God's voice must speak.

When John the Baptist was taken out of the picture, his disciples became disciples of Jesus. This revealed true humility and greatness. He was, as he said, "the friend of the bridegroom . . . [who] rejoiceth greatly because of the bridegroom's voice: this my joy therefore is fulfilled" (3:29). He prepared his disciples to follow Jesus; the Son of God was the important one in John's eyes. "And I, if I be lifted up from the earth," Jesus said, "will draw all men unto me" (12:32). John the Baptist lifted up Jesus Christ in sincerity, humility, and righteousness.

Prisoner of Purpose

John spent the closing days of his life in prison, but he was a *prisoner of purpose*. It seems strange to think of this thundering outdoor man imprisoned in a dungeon. Why? For preaching the gospel. Every time someone asks, "Why do the righteous suffer?" I think of John the Baptist, who was beheaded for preaching righteousness. Daniel also suffered because of his righteousness. The magnificent roll call of Old Testament saints in Hebrews 11—all of them suffered for righeousness' sake.

The more righteous you are, the more likely it is that you will suffer for it. You do not become the enemy of unrighteous people until you declare yourself wholeheartedly on the side of God. When Christ becomes the one passion of your life, and those around you do not share that conviction, then you are at odds.

John did not cut his message to fit his hearers. He dared to preach the unwelcome judgment of God even to Herod the king. "It is not lawful for thee to have thy brother's wife," he told Herod bluntly (Mark 6:18). This offended Herod, who had John put in prison. Preaching the righteousness of God will always make enemies.

Herod's wife did not declare the reason she hated John and wanted him beheaded, but she managed to arrange his death. It was the cruel injustice of a sinful world that God's great messenger should die because of the jealousy of an evil woman and at the request of a half-naked dancing girl. Because a man had become so drunk that his senses were dulled, because a woman so flaunted herself before a lustful group, John suffered martyrdom. The scene was evil beyond description, beyond imagination, beyond decency.

Thus, John's ringing voice was stilled. But there are some words that have to be said; there are some truths that have to be preached; there are some things that are worth dying for. John believed that. Just as Jesus steadfastly set his face toward Jerusalem and the cross, just as the apostle Paul desired to preach at Rome even though he knew he risked his life, so John the Baptist preached God's message to Herod—and it cost him his head.

We also may face violence and hatred from those who disagree with our message from God. The world reckons success by popularity—but not the Lord. In his sight, it is far better to be faithful than it is to be popular. God needs a distinctive voice like John's today—a voice of certainty, a voice of truth, a voice speaking for God. He doesn't need an echo, he needs a voice!

"What this parish needs," said sarcastic, old Thomas Carlyle about his little English village, "is a parson that has had an experience with God himself."

The voice of John the Baptist was clear and definite, but it was silenced. Now it is about time that we lifted up our voices, willing to pay the price, if necessary. You may say, "Yes, but I will have to go it alone." John the Baptist spent a long, long time in the wilderness. He was lonely, but he was never alone, for God was with him.

Today we know Jesus Christ a little better because of the message of John the Baptist who pointed to the coming

Lamb of God. John revered him. John trusted him. John proclaimed him with clarity, simplicity, and dedication.

We may be alone, we may be only a voice in the wilderness. We may find ourselves laughed at, as John was—or beheaded. But we remember the Bible says that by the foolishness of preaching men shall be saved. Today, also, as in New Testament days, "If the trumpet give an uncertain sound, who shall prepare himself to the battle" of righteousness? (1 Cor. 14:8)

3
Maiden Mother

(Luke 1:26–56)

"Therefore the Lord himself shall give you a sign," declared Isaiah the prophet more than seven hundred years before the birth of Jesus. "Behold, a virgin shall conceive, and bear a son, and shall call his name Immanuel" (7:14).

In the first chapter of Luke we find the beautiful account of the fulfilment of that prophecy: "In the sixth month the angel Gabriel was sent from God unto a city of Galilee, named Nazareth, to a virgin espoused to a man whose name was Joseph, of the house of David; and the virgin's name was Mary" (vv. 26–27).

"Mary, the mother of Jesus, has not had fair treatment from either Catholics or Protestants," said Dr. A. T. Robertson, a great Greek theologian among Southern Baptists.

We should neither deify Mary nor detract from her memory. The proper emphasis was given the night her Son was born. The shepherds came to see where the child lay. The Scriptures say they all worshiped him. So ought we also to worship him.

However, any serious student of history knows that

through the centuries there has been sharp division concerning that scene in the stable. During the first two or three hundred years, there seemed to be no problem: worship centered upon the newborn babe, the Son of God, the Messiah who died and rose again. Jesus was the promised one, born of a human mother, but without human father, the one who was prophesied in the Holy Scriptures.

The worship of Mary began to develop in the third and fourth centuries. The legend grew up that Mary also was of virgin conception and birth—to make her fit to bear the holy child. In 1854, the Catholic Church proclaimed it official dogma. In 1950, a further dogma was issued that Mary ascended bodily into heaven, that like her Son, her body was saved from corruption so that she could be co-redemptrix. This theory destroys the doctrine of the direct fatherhood of God for Jesus Christ.

Marian theology is foreign to the Word of God. According to the New Testament, it is not necessary to go through Mary or anyone else to get to the heart of Jesus.

"What think ye of Christ?" was the question of New Testament times, not, "What think ye of Mary?" Jesus turned to his own disciples and asked, "What think ye of Christ?" The emphasis of the New Testament has always been on the Saviour. However, we cannot ignore the fact that some people have taken half-truths and tried to expand them into important doctrines. In almost every picture we see of the family of Jesus, Mary and Joseph are depicted with halos around their heads. It would be well indeed to ask, "What does the Bible say?"

A Miraculous Birth

First of all, the Bible says very clearly that the birth of Jesus was a miracle. When the angel Gabriel appeared to Mary, he said, "The Holy Ghost shall come upon thee, and the power of the Highest shall overshadow thee: therefore also that holy thing which shall be born of thee shall be called the Son of God" (Luke 1:35). The fact that Jesus was the only child ever born of a virgin mother one has a right to question. But to deny it raises a lot more questions, questions no one knows completely how to answer. The question raised by the virgin birth can be answered only on the basis of God's Word, and the fact that Jesus was virgin-born is definitely taught in the Scriptures. The first promise of God is in the third chapter of Genesis, when he said that the seed of the woman should bruise the head of the serpent.

Matthew stated positively that Jesus was virgin-born: "Before they came together, she was found with child of the Holy Ghost" (1:18). Luke also emphasized the virgin birth, and in even greater detail. John pointed up the virgin birth of Jesus by emphasis on the Lord's heavenly origin: "In the beginning was the Word, and the Word was with God, and the Word was God. The Word was made flesh, and dwelt among us" (John 1:1,14). Mark did not begin with the birth of Jesus. He began with Christ's public ministry, but his opening words were, "The beginning of the gospel of Jesus Christ, the Son of God" (1:1).

In the Bible, there are twenty-three references to Mary, sixteen of which concern the birth of Jesus. When he was twelve, she found him in the Temple. During his ministry, she attended the wedding feast at Cana and, with his brothers, visited him another time when he was preaching. Twice Jesus is referred to by others as "the son of Mary." With John, the beloved disciple, Mary stood near the cross when her Son was crucified, and in the first chapter of Acts she is listed as among those who prayed and waited for Pentecost.

Those who traced the genealogy of Jesus in the Scriptures give evidence again and again that Jesus was virgin-born. Of course, we would expect atheists like Thomas Payne, Voltaire, Ingersoll, and others to say that he was nothing more than an illegitimate child. "I do not believe in the virgin birth of Christ," wrote Matthew Arnold, "because it involves a miracle, and miracles do not happen." How can a man take it upon himself to declare that miracles don't happen? How can he set limits on the power of God?

Mary herself faced great scorn, and was certainly deeply hurt by slander. Great embarrassment was heaped upon this young girl. Those who write historical novels have conjectured that her child was the son of a Roman soldier who passed that way. But we would not expect to hear such things from the clergy, nor from the church pew, nor from men who consider themselves educated Christian gentlemen.

Others try to minimize the problem by saying that it makes no difference. Jesus could have become the Son of God at a later date, they say. Don't you believe it! The

Bible is either the Word of God or the words of men. It is either divinely inspired, or it is not. If it is divinely inspired, then we can believe Matthew, Mark, Luke, John, Isaiah, and the other prophets of God.

When the angel appeared to Mary, she asked in surprise, "How can this be, seeing I know not a man?" When Joseph noticed her condition he wondered, "How can this be?" Joseph, her betrothed husband, loved Mary deeply, but that did not make it any easier for him to believe her story. It was incredible! Nothing like this had ever happened before, and Joseph felt he had to face reality. But the angel came to him with a message from God (Matt. 1:20–21). Then Joseph believed and took Mary as his wife.

Blessed Among Women

The angel addressed Mary, the mother of Jesus: "Hail, thou that art highly favoured, the Lord is with thee: blessed art thou among women."

What about this little maiden whom God picked to be the mother of Jesus? What kind of woman was she? What kind of home did she have? What about her childhood?

It is thought by some that she was an orphan. Bible history does not mention her mother or father; only legends tell us about them. If Mary was an orphan, perhaps she worked as a housemaid. What could a young girl thirteen to sixteen years old do to make a living unless she was a servant? In the Oriental world, woman's lot was hard.

I doubt that, as some have said, every girl in Palestine looked for the coming of the Messiah and hoped to be his mother. It is only a supposition, a legend not even hinted at in the New Testament.

God doesn't look on the outside of people, as men do. He looked into the heart of this girl, Mary, and evidently he found there just what he wanted—blameless character, humility, and faith. But although Mary's character was blameless, there came a time when her reputation was brought into question. She fled to the house of Elizabeth, her cousin, to hide from all the gossip. As Mary came into the room, Elizabeth knew immediately that God had visited Mary. Elizabeth may have been as a mother to the young girl and trained her in the arts of motherhood.

Mary probably endured a harsh and cruel time. Joseph dealt kindly with her, but the neighbors probably thought exactly what she thought they did.

It was then that Caesar, far off in Rome, decreed a census in Palestine. Joseph, being of the lineage of David, had to go to Bethlehem. Did Mary ride a donkey? Legend more than history tells us that she did—we cannot be sure. She may have walked every trudging step of the way.

When they came to Bethlehem, they went from inn to inn, from house to house, seeking lodging. Everyone was very busy. Everybody had plans of their own. "Well!" you may think indignantly, "if I had lived there it would have been different. I would have done something wonderful for them!" I'm afraid such assertions from us are as much out of place as Peter's when he said to the Lord, "Everybody else may forsake you, but I'm going to stick with you to the end if it kills me!"

For Peter was the first one to deny his Lord. It is easy for us to look back and, knowing about his miracles, his death, his resurrection, sit in a comfortable church and say what we would have done in such an emergency.

We would have done then just what we are doing now. What are we doing about the children around us that need clothes and food and help? "If you have done it unto the least of these, my brethren," Jesus said, "you have done it unto me." If we have not done it unto others, he would say to us today, we would not have done it unto him. If we are selfish, we would have been selfish at that hour. If we do nothing for the unfortunate today, we would have done nothing for the unfortunate family of Joseph then.

For never was a family in more unfortunate circumstances than Mary and Joseph when they came to Bethlehem. Far from home and friends, they had no one to help them. There was no attending physician. Swaddling clothes were the best gift they had for the expected baby. The whole world sings now of the time when the King was cradled in a stable. But are we making the lot of humanity any better now? Or is life still like that empty stable—no food, no Christ, no hope?

It took a lot of faith for this little maiden mother to believe what God's messenger told her. She was so childlike that she accepted the angel's word, so womanlike that she wished for something a little better than a stable for her baby. In the Temple, forty days later, an aged priest told her, "A sword shall pierce through thy own soul also." Many of Jesus' sufferings also hurt his mother.

I would hasten to say that the greatest thing that happened that first Christmas was that God came down from heaven. I do not understand how, though I believe it, the great God of the universe should have been willing to imprison himself in human flesh, subject to dirt, pain, tears, hunger, hate. But the great truth of the Incarnation is that Jesus, God's Son, God himself, was in that manger-cradle. To believe it takes all the faith that I have.

Mary a Mystery?

What about the mystery of this woman, Mary? How should we regard her? If we look to Jesus as our example, we find that he regarded her with respect, reverence, and tenderness. He provided for her. Even when he was dying, he said to his disciple, John, "Behold thy mother," and to her, "Behold thy son."

John took her to his own house and provided for her the rest of her life. He didn't have to, but he loved Jesus enough to do it for him. Because he loved Jesus, he loved Mary enough that he was willing to do it for her sake.

Sometimes we lose touch with reality in considering spiritual things. We live in the material world until we forget the intangibles of life. We feel that the more we possess, the better we are. John became a better man because he did what Jesus asked him to do. The woman who broke the alabaster box became a better woman because she did what her heart told her to do.

It happens to all of us. We make a plea for foreign missions. We make a plea for home missions. We say, "Do it for their sake." But rather, we should do it for our own sake. If we do not, Jesus will ask someone else to do it. God will raise up another church or another preacher or another deacon or another Christian worker. We had better serve the Lord while we can—for our own sake.

We cannot place Mary as a fourth in the Godhead, next to the Trinity. Men come into fellowship with God only through Jesus Christ, his Son. We do not have to seek the intercession of another. The heart of Jesus is always open to all who call on him.

The thing the early church preached most was the resurrection of Jesus Christ. From the time that Jesus appeared to his disciples in the upper room, and more especially from the day of Pentecost, there was one supreme emphasis: Jesus Christ came forth from the grave. He is victor over death! He is alive forevermore!

Where is Mary when the Bible last mentions her? The book of Acts places her among those faithful followers of the risen Christ who prayed and believed and received the Holy Spirit. She did not put herself in any position of power or authority; she looked to her Son. This is the true message of the gospel—neither a creed, nor the writings of man, but the Word of God which has been given to guide the Christian.

Mary would be the first to say, "I have no right to adoration." For it was she who sang, rejoicing, God "hath regarded the low estate of his handmaiden: for, behold, from henceforth all generations shall call me blessed" (Luke 1:48).

4
Forgotten Father

(Matthew 1:18–25)

On a visit to Bethlehem we were staying in a little hotel no larger than a good-sized two-story house. Upstairs, our tiny bedroom, with only one window, wasn't much bigger than the nook at home where we have our piano. We were nearly suffocating. It was a Saturday evening in July. From the dining room downstairs, unexpectedly there floated up the beautiful strains of a Christmas carol.

Many of our churches know about "Christmas in August," because the children bring gifts in midsummer to send to our missionaries so that children in foreign lands may receive them by Christmas. But at first it seemed strangely out of season to hear Christmas carols in July. The music drew us down to the dining room where we stood around the wall with other tourists. Then we realized how appropriate it was to sing Christmas carols in Bethlehem, even in July. In the beauty of the Christmas music we were able to capture again something of the love, warmth, joy—and also the problems that existed there when Jesus was born.

Matthew gives us an insight into the problem of Joseph,

a carpenter living in Nazareth. "Then Joseph her husband, being a just man, and not willing to make her a public example, was minded to put her away privily" (v. 19).

Joseph was a man of the Judean hills, a descendant of David. Bethlehem was his ancestral home. Mary's family's home was also Bethlehem. But Joseph, being a carpenter by trade and perhaps finding it difficult to earn a living there, had left Bethlehem and gone to Nazareth to live. Maybe the same problem drove the family of Mary from Bethlehem to Nazareth, for carpenters and workmen often followed one building boom after another.

A Difficult Decision

Life wasn't all starlight and music that first Christmas night. It wasn't peaceful and sweet to Mary and Joseph. Their difficulties and discomforts were frighteningly real.

Joseph had been faced with a distressing problem. He was engaged to Mary, a young maiden—probably a teenager, because early marriage for girls was the custom. When we read that he was "espoused" to Mary, it meant that they had made a legal and binding contract to marry. It was the next thing to marriage itself. To have the bonds of engagement broken, they had to go through certain public ceremonies. It wasn't the way we think of engagements today, where a promise to wed seems to mean very little. Breaking an engagement then was not a matter of having a fuss and pulling off the ring and saying, "We're through!"

A dowry might already have been given to the bridegroom-to-be. Likely, Mary had little to offer, but she was definitely set apart in the sight of the community to become the wife of Joseph, who may have been an older man. If he should say, "I do not wish this young woman to be my wife," he needed to give some definite reason. He had to have something almost sufficient to be grounds for divorce, as if they had already been married. Thus Joseph had a difficult problem, especially as he was a good man, a godly man, a kind man.

Joseph is often neglected in the Christmas story. Perhaps we do not ponder enough about Joseph. He does not belong in the picture as the natural father of Jesus, yet we ought to feel a warm respect for this man who was such a faithful foster-father. Jesus worked at the carpenter's bench with Joseph and evidently learned much from this good man. The respect that Jesus had for a good day's work he learned from Joseph. God made no mistake when he picked this man to give his Son the guidance of an earthly father.

The Scriptures, for the most part, are silent about Joseph. This very silence allows us to speculate on how he must have felt in the face of such difficulties.

After the angel had come to Mary, she had gone to Elizabeth and stayed some three months—perhaps until after the baby John was born. When she came back, it was obvious that she was with child. She offered no explanation to Joseph. If she had, I'm not sure he would have believed it. Would you? What anguish and heartbreak for him!

Then God spoke to Joseph. God always knows our suffering, and suffering comes to us all. Joseph had already decided on the best way known to him and proved that he was a good and kind man.

"Joseph," the angel of God said, "it is difficult for you to believe what I have to say. But Mary has not known a man—this child is of the Holy Spirit. Go on and take her as your wife."

Obeying God, Joseph went through with the marriage ceremony as soon as possible. From that time, when God had something to say about the safety of Jesus, the angel appeared to Joseph. He was the head of the family. He had believed God and taken the responsibility. He had proved himself obedient, and the Lord rewarded his faith.

A Concerned Father

Although Jesus was not his own son, Joseph showed parental concern. He cared for his foster-son as he did for his other children. He shared the dreams and hopes and fears of Mary; they were able to talk about what had happened to both of them. Having to go to Bethlehem for the census, Joseph took Mary with him—perhaps to protect her from what might be said about her.

Later, when Herod was seeking to find the one born "King of the Jews," the angel came to Joseph again. "Take the young child into Egypt for safety," the angel said. Joseph didn't argue with God. The safety of this child that God had committed to Joseph's care became the first thought of his life. That he was a good and kind man he showed in his dealings with Mary; but he was also a godly man, for no longer did he put material things first. If the child Jesus was in danger, he would do what he could to protect him.

Joseph did not say—he did not even think, "If this is the Son of God, why can't God take care of him?" Instead, Joseph took the attitude, "God has given me this responsibility. I'll take care of it." What wonderful faithfulness!

Joseph and Mary and Jesus stayed in Egypt for quite a while—perhaps several years. Then the angel of God came and said, "Joseph, Herod is dead. It is all right for you to go back to Nazareth." How they made a living in Egypt, we do not know. I am sure there were questions in Joseph's mind about going back to Nazareth. He remembered the cutting remarks. Such things aren't easy to forget. But at the command of God he went back, taking Mary and Jesus.

Joseph and the firstborn son of Mary stood at the carpenter's bench together and the boy learned the toil of the laborer. The concern of Joseph for this child and for the welfare of his wife, is one of the inspiring things we should remember at the Christmas season. No child could have had a better father.

A Good Teacher

Joseph's part in the story of Jesus shows us a man on a patient journey through life, taking care of his family. In the Temple, Simeon told Mary, "A sword shall pierce through thy own soul also" (Luke 2:35). Some swords pierced Joseph's heart, too.

The first time Jesus preached in Nazareth, people looked at him and asked, "Is this the carpenter's son?" Knowing that Jesus came from the wrong side of the tracks, so to speak, the Judeans questioned sneeringly, "Can any good come out of Nazareth?" It wasn't easy for Joseph to take the things that were said against his wife and the boy Jesus. But Joseph was patient in all his dealings. He taught Jesus to be a good workman and to take responsibility as oldest son in the family. When Jesus was twelve years of age, his mother and Joseph found him in the Temple talking to the teachers. This is the last time Joseph is mentioned.

I'd like to think that many of the illustrations Jesus used in his ministry came out of Joseph's carpentry shop. "Take my yoke upon you," he said. He knew how to make yokes easy for the oxen to wear; he knew how to shape them to fit just right. He had heard the talk of the farmers; he knew the problems of planting and reaping. He probably carried water for his family, as was the custom for the oldest child.

Surely no mother could have had a better son than Jesus. When she found him in the Temple, he asked, "Know ye not that I must be about my Father's business?" But that indicated no lack of respect on his part. He minded his mother and obeyed Joseph, doing all the things that a good son ought to do in the home. Secular history indicates that Joseph died when Jesus was about eighteen years of age. This we cannot be sure of. We know only that before Jesus began his public ministry, Mary became a widow.

Jesus' Family

What about the other children in the family?

At least six children besides Jesus are mentioned in Matthew 13:55—four brothers and two (or more) sisters. James, who wrote the book called by his name in the New Testament, was a half brother of Jesus. And I'd like to think that Joseph was the second son of Mary, named after his father. Then there was Judas—not Judas Iscariot (Judas was a perfectly good name until Judas Iscariot tarnished it). Simon was another. As the word "sisters" is in the plural, there were at least two, maybe more, but none is mentioned by name.

One day early in Jesus' ministry when he was teaching in Galilee, he was informed, "Lord, your mother and your brothers are here and want to see you."

"Who is my mother and who are my brethren?" he replied. "Whosoever shall do the will of my Father which is in heaven, the same is my brother, and sister, and mother" (Matt. 12:50).

In later days, a woman tried to praise Jesus by saying, "Blessed is the woman who bore you." Jesus rebuked her with the answer, "Yea rather, blessed are they that hear the word of God, and keep it" (Luke 11:28). He cut all physical ties to magnify spiritual rather than physical relationships.

But his brother James, after the risen Lord appeared to him, followed Jesus and became the first pastor of the church in Jerusalem. It seems that Jesus, when he appeared to James, did not speak a word. When James saw him and felt his loving and pleading gaze, he believed. He recognized him as the divine Son of God. James didn't doubt like Thomas, who declared, "Except I shall see in his hands the print of the nails, . . . I will not believe."

Jesus evidently did not appear to his mother after his resurrection. Whether he thought it was too much to appear to her as the risen Son of God, I do not know. In the later days of his ministry, he began to talk more and more about our brother-and-sister relationship in the family of God.

To realize that we are the sons of God, joint heirs with Jesus Christ in all the spiritual riches of God, is nearly incredible. Can you believe it? It is such a miracle—just as great a miracle as Jesus' birth, or his raising the dead, or his own resurrection. Yet he said that we also become the children of God when we believe in him.

By adoption, we have been brought into the family of God. We had no claim on God, because we had sinned against his love and his laws. But the loving Son of God came to earth to bring us back, like the poor lost sheep. Oh, how grateful we are that we can be part of the family of God!

5

Bethlehem's Birth

(Matthew 1:18–25)

A Jew named Matthew worked for the Romans as a tax-gatherer. A clerical man, he was familiar with the tax procedure of those days, which kept track of people by their families and ancestors rather than by social security numbers. He began his account of the life of Jesus Christ with a genealogy which is evidently that of Joseph.

Matthew was called by Jesus personally from his tax-collecting job to be a disciple. After the Lord's ascension, he wrote out very carefully the narrative as he had received the impression of the Holy Spirit. Matthew realized that people might have difficulty believing the stupendous story he was going to tell them. After the genealogy, which traced Jesus' legal descent (Joseph being Jesus' foster-father) back to Abraham, he inserted an explanatory sentence: "Now, the birth of Jesus Christ was on this wise."

What Matthew had to tell was so startling and magnificent that he wanted the full and credulous attention of his readers. Upon their acceptance of his account of the birth of Jesus depended his whole story of the one born to be King. If Jesus was not the true Son of God, the crucifixion was nothing more than a tragedy among many tragedies of history. The resurrection would be beyond belief.

Paul wrote, in his great resurrection chapter, "If Christ be not raised, your faith is vain; ye are yet in your sins" (1 Cor. 15:17). Unless Christ rose from the dead, those who have died are lost; there is no victory over the grave, no hope at all! If we have believed in a miraculous resurrection and there is no resurrection, we are, indeed, "of all men most miserable!" What creed is worth subscribing to which does not affirm that Jesus Christ is the divinely conceived, unique Son of God?

The testimony of many that he was the divine King sent from God, the evidence of his sinless life, and the circumstances of his death and resurrection assure us that we have every reason in the world to believe that his birth was miraculous.

While we are considering his birth in Bethlehem, let us not for a moment think that Jesus Christ did not exist before that first Christmas. Jesus was the only begotten Son of God *before* the foundation of the world. The first verse of the Bible uses the word "God" in the plural, indicating the involvement of the whole Trinity, the Godhead, in creating the heavens and the earth. Before the foundation of the earth was laid, Jesus was the eternal Word of God. The Incarnation was the method God chose to enter the world to save mankind. The birth of Jesus is recognized as the watershed of history. "He who in eternity rested upon the bosom of a Father without a mother," wrote Dr.

M. E. Dodd, "in time rested upon the bosom of a mother without a father."

The celebration of his birth is such a joyous occasion because it is the birthday of hope. It is the beginning of eternal joy in the human scheme of things. Because it is the beginning of hope, we can grasp hold of God and go on hoping throughout the year.

A Life of Miracles

The life of Jesus in this world began with a miraculous birth. His ministry was characterized by miracles. His time on earth ended with the miracles of his resurrection and ascension. We worship a miracle-working God. We cannot discuss the birth of Jesus without using the word "miraculous." There is no other word that describes it so exactly. His was a miraculous birth. To call it simply a supernatural birth is not sufficient. Isaac had a supernatural birth; his parents were far past the age of having children. John the Baptist had a supernatural birth, also. But the word "supernatural" does not apply to the virgin birth of Jesus Christ.

Why is it difficult to believe that God could perform a miraculous conception? Everything that exists is a miracle of God. The bodies in which we live are remarkable. The psalmist said, "I am fearfully and wonderfully made" (Psalm 139:14). It was a miracle when God "formed man of the dust of the ground" (Gen. 2:7). He created a beautifully functioning physical body in which human life could be tabernacled.

Miracles Do Happen

Who is man to declare that it is not reasonable or possible for God to perform a miracle in creating another human body without natural generation? What is a miracle? A miracle is defined as something contrary to the laws of nature as we understand them. But do we have all understanding? Does mankind possess all knowledge? No, there are many unknowables in life.

We have to go back only one generation to demonstrate this. Some years ago it would have been thought incredible that a man could talk into a microphone and people behind closed doors far away, or traveling down a broad highway in a speeding car could hear his voice clearly. Our great-grandfathers would have said, "What utter fools!" of those who prophesied such a thing.

A few years ago, to claim that one could take a tape and record words on it and put it on a shelf until years later, then get it down and put it on a machine and the voice still be there, clear and recognizable—our ancestors would have said, "What a wild fancy!"

If many of us, as children, had been told that the day would come when we would not only be able to listen to a human voice across thousands of miles but to see things happening on the other side of the earth, our reaction would have been, "Impossible!"

Perhaps one day the world may learn even more of the secrets of God's universe. But let us understand and believe that we serve a miracle-working God who created that universe. He is never behind the times—although our conception of him may be—because to him there is no time. He knows not only the past and present but also the future that seems too vague to us.

God's Mysterious Way

The birth of Christ, though prophesied by many in great detail, was still mysterious. We simply cannot understand it. Here one who had no earthly father was born of woman in Bethlehem, the city of David.

Bethlehem means "house of bread." Strangely enough, he who was the Bread of life was born in the house of bread—but almost on the outside. For Bethlehem did not have room for him who was the Bread of life sent from God.

Luke, the writer of the Third Gospel, was a physician. Surely no one would have more difficulty than a medical man like Luke believing Mary's story. Yet Luke gave the genealogy of Jesus' mother. He traced by inspiration, in greatest detail, the birth of Jesus, using the words that came to him, using the knowledge that was given to him. We tremble when we realize that God did all this for us.

When I consider the mysterious birth of Jesus, our Saviour, the greatest trouble I have is not *how,* but *why!* It is easier to understand how God could do it than to understand why God *would* do it. We are awed before the Incarnation. "And the Word was made flesh, and dwelt among us," John declared. Jesus came down from heaven's glory. Why should he? The only time we find the word Emmanuel in the New Testament is in Matthew's narrative (1:23;

cf. Isa. 8:10). It is an old Hebrew word meaning "God with us." In his incredible announcement, the angel declared that God is no longer far away, he is *with us!*

"God's in his heaven:/All's right with the world," wrote Robert Browning. I appreciate his poetry and I like these lines; but if God had remained only in heaven, nothing could be right with the world. For God that day did not limit himself to his own abode. Emmanuel, "God with us," came down to walk on earth in the body of a man. He hungered, he thirsted, he suffered—God in us, before us, beside us. Life is bearable, because it is sharable with God. We need to realize that the same Emmanuel, the same God who came to us on that first Christmas day, is with us still.

The Birthday of Hope

Somehow we have the idea around Christmas time that we must hurry to send out cards and packages; when our cards are looked at and our packages opened, Christmas is over. But that is not true. Christmas is hope's birthday. Christmas is "God with us": Isaiah's Immanuel (7:14), identified in Jesus Christ our Lord, will never leave us. "[When] I depart, I will send him [the Holy Spirit] unto you" (John 16:7). He will be with us all the while. "For he hath said, I will never leave thee, nor forsake thee" (Heb. 13:5). Christmas lasts all year because God stays with us forever. "God with us" is the good news of the gospel.

Not very many people in Bethlehem were conscious of what happened that first Christmas when God came down. Probably some heard the cry of an infant, but if someone had said to them, "Messiah is born," they would have shrugged their shoulders in disbelief. As far as they were concerned, nothing important happened that night.

Yet God was born, though they were unaware of it. Jesus later died physically and was buried physically. But his spirit, which could not die, picked up that dead body and transformed it to live forever. "God *is* a Spirit," Jesus said on one occasion, "and they that worship him must worship him in spirit and in truth" (John 4:24). Isaiah said, incredible as it may seem, that God's promised deliverer would be Immanuel, God with us.

Many people today also ignore the divine meaning of the drama of Bethlehem: "Immanuel—God with us!" He is with us still; he is by our side.

Magnificent Morning Star

The only word that truly describes the birth, life, death, and resurrection of Jesus is magnificence. He limited himself to time and space. One of the Trinity, a member of the Godhead, he was omnipotent, omnipresent, and eternal. Triumphant and glorious Deity, he identified himself with his people on earth. His advent was foretold by prophets. His birth was announced by angels. His life was described by the Gospels. His purity was undeniable; he met temptation and conquered Satan. He endured death but arose again in the form of a man and now he lives forever.

In the crises of life, one person often comforts another with, "God knows." It is not an idle phrase—God *does* know! My loved one may be dead—God knows! His beloved Son was nailed to a cross. My loved one has been condemned by others. God knows! Fever? God knows! Sweat in a carpenter's shop? God knows! Hunger and thirst? God knows!

"Immanuel" is a name we should use more often to remind ourselves that God is still with us. He is with us now in the magnificence of the presence of Jesus in our midst— the lily of the valley, the bright and morning star, the fairest of ten thousand. He, the very essence of God in human flesh, is with us now.

We ought to be just as interested in that birth two thousand years ago as were the shepherds who were amazed that night on the hillside because of the good news told them by the angels: "Unto you is born this day in the city of David a Saviour." For if Jesus was not the virgin-born Son of God, then he was not the Son of God at all. And if he wasn't the Son of God, he could not be our sinless Saviour and we would have no Saviour!

By faith we come and say with Matthew, "Now the birth of Jesus Christ was on this wise." He became "God with us." God's voice spoke from heaven declaring, "This is my beloved Son, in whom I am well pleased."

Down the centuries Jesus Christ has walked with his people, and he is near and dear to us this very hour in a way he could not be to those who stood around the manger and worshiped the newborn child.

6

Angelic Announcement

(Luke 1:11–15, 26–30; 2:8–15)

"We need Christmas," said Harold Cook Phillips a long time ago. "Christmas is like a beautiful island rising from the turbulent waters, with man looking for a place to land."

If it were not for Christmas, would there ever be a cease-fire? Would there ever be a letup from the harshness of the dog-eat-dog world? Would men, in their pursuit of fame and fortune ever take time for others who have needs —not just for charity, but for a reason to live again? The spirit with which we give is far more important than the amount. We should help a needy child with the hope that we might strike a chord of responsiveness, that he might raise himself above his poverty and find a sense of worth-whileness, a sense of purpose, even a sense of mission in life.

It is not a matter of the charity which we give, but of the manner in which we serve.

We do need Christmas desperately! We need its music, for it is the sweetest music under heaven. We need its star of promise. We need its mystic wonder. We need its cheer.

We need the angel's message of hope, "Peace on earth, good will toward men."

"Messengers of God"

Christmas is a wonderful time to think about angels, for they are mentioned several times in the accounts of the birth of Christ.

The very thought of angels fills us with wonder. Yet some people say they have difficulty believing in angels. I have no difficulty at all accepting the profound things of God in simplicity—maybe that's the difference between my childlike mind, with its inquisitiveness, and the closed minds of those who cannot accept the mysterious, infinite things of God.

In the order of creation, God is always above and beyond, before and after, the Alpha and Omega, the beginning and end of everything. This earth and its inhabitants were evidently not the first nor only creation of God. Other creations are mentioned briefly in the Scriptures.

Angels are evidently a separate order of created beings. Some are called archangels, and some are called by name— Gabriel and Michael, for instance. All of them are ministering spirits sent from God. When they have appeared visibly, they have been seen in the form of men.

"Angel" is from a Greek word that means messenger. Angels are the messengers of God. Will we ever be angels? No. The closest we will come is that we may be sent by God to do his will or perform some task for him, and thus we will fulfil a similar function as messengers.

When Jesus came to live among us, it was said about him that he "took upon him the form of a servant, and was made in the likeness of men" (Phil. 2:7). Also, "Thou madest him a little [for a little time] lower than the angels" (Heb. 2:7). Angels have a higher position than mankind, but redeemed men of the "new creation" will excel them. The Bible says that we shall judge angels. Although they do not sin as men sin, the Bible speaks of fallen angels, and Satan seems to be their leader.

Angels were never intended to be objects of our worship; rather, in every case where we find them mentioned in God's Word they have been ministering spirits, assisting and instructing men, leading in the adoration and worship of God. They are mentioned many times in the Bible, but there are four occurrences in the New Testament which relate to the birth of the Saviour.

Zacharias' Anticipation

First, an angel came to Zacharias the priest and gave him a message that caused great anticipation. He and his wife, Elizabeth, an elder cousin of Mary of Nazareth, were growing old and they had no children.

Zacharias left his house one day to perform his service at the Temple of God. Each day the necessary duties were portioned out among the priests by casting lots. One would have the privilege of burning the incense at the holy altar of God. That was a day of days in a priest's life; only once in his lifetime could he have that special privilege.

I don't know how a priest thought—much like preachers,

perhaps. I'm sure he felt unworthy, but I imagine there was in his heart that day a prayer, as in the heart of every priest who had not served there, "O God, let me have the privilege, ere I die, of standing in the holy place to burn incense to God."

Zacharias must have been very thankful and happy the day it fell his lot to burn the incense. While he was performing this holy and beautiful function, an angel appeared to him, standing on the right side of the altar of incense. Zacharias was very frightened. Fear always falls on men when they are surrounded by the glory of heaven on earth.

"Fear not, Zacharias," the angel said, "for thy prayer is heard; and thy wife Elisabeth shall bear thee a son, and thou shalt call his name John" (Luke 1:13). He was to be the Forerunner of the Messiah and a very special servant of God. The name John meant "one who is given." Truly a baby was a great gift of God to this elderly couple.

But Zacharias was incredulous. "Whereby shall I know this?" he demanded, "for I am an old man, and my wife well stricken in years."

He reacted much like we would have reacted, not only with fear but with difficulty in believing. What would we do if we saw an angel? I sometimes fear we have lost the ability to apprehend spiritual things. Are we sensitive to the Holy Spirit whom the Lord promised would be our ever-present guide?

Zacharias demanded a sign: "Whereby shall I know this?" It is better not to ask God for a sign. We should take

God at his word and start performing his work. Because Zacharias did not believe, the angel said, "Thou shalt be dumb, and not able to speak, until the day that these things shall be performed."

He made his way back home and Elizabeth immediately asked what was the matter. But no words could pass his lips. Finally, he wrote down for her this thing that had happened to him.

There are many similarities between the birth of John and the birth of Jesus. Each birth was foretold, and it was declared that many should rejoice. It was a time of great joy and festivity when John was born to this elderly couple who had no children.

Wherever there are angels, there is music. After the child was born, Zacharias recovered his speech and his first words were a hymn of outstanding beauty and joy: "Blessed be the Lord God of Israel; for he hath visited and redeemed his people, . . . And thou, child, shalt be called the prophet of the Highest: for thou shalt go before the face of the Lord to prepare his ways; to give knowledge of salvation unto his people by the remission of their sins" (Luke 1:68–76).

The birth of John, as well as the birth of Jesus, was uniquely a gift of God. John's birth prepared the way of the Lord. Each played a part in God's plan to bring us the way of salvation. Each was born, not to magnify himself, but to point to another—in John's case to Jesus, and in Jesus' case to the Father. Even though our births were not announced by angels, our lives should point to the Lord.

Gabriel's Announcement

The angel Gabriel came to earth with another announcement a few months later. This annunciation was to a wisp of a girl, a virgin who lived in Nazareth and was engaged to a man named Joseph.

It is a tradition that every girl in Israel prayed to be the mother of the Messiah. But history gives us no reason to believe it and the Bible doesn't mention it. When Mary realized that she was the one chosen to bear the Messiah, she was greatly amazed and fearful.

Every time an angel appeared in the Bible, the first words he uttered were usually, "Fear not!" Every time something spiritual happens, something glorious, something joyously unexpected, we become frightened. It is too much for us, it seems. We try to explain it in nonspiritual terms. When the Holy Spirit descended on the day of Pentecost, Peter had to tell the people, "We are not drunk like you say we are." It is difficult to understand the things of the Spirit. We are never prepared and we have to lean on secular words to transmit the message of the Spirit.

The angel spoke to Mary, saying, "Hail, thou that art highly favored, the Lord is with thee: blessed art thou among women" (Luke 1:28). She was so frightened he had to repeat, "Fear not, Mary: for thou hast found favour with God" (v. 30).

Although puzzled and perplexed, Mary was not unbelieving like Zacharias. Her question was not, "How can *I* know this?" but "*How can* this thing be?" She pondered what she should tell her parents. What could she tell

Joseph? What should she believe herself? "How can this thing be?"

St. Bernard declared that here are three miracles: first, that God and man should be joined in this child; second, that a mother should be a virgin; third, that Mary should have had faith to believe this mystery would be accomplished in her.

Mary's fear blossomed into faith. From her lips came the magnificent song as she rejoiced with Elizabeth: "My soul doth magnify the Lord, and my spirit hath rejoiced in God my Saviour. . . . For, behold, from henceforth all generations shall call me blessed" (vv. 46–48).

Where angels have been, song is not far behind. Martin Luther wrote, "To understand this sacred hymn of praise, we need to understand that Mary is speaking on the basis of her own experience, in which she was enlightened and instructed by the Holy Spirit."

Joseph's Appreciation

Then the angel had another message, one for Joseph, the espoused bridegroom of Mary. It was received by him, not with song, but at least with great *appreciation*. Perhaps his song was a sigh of silence. His heart was painfully perplexed when he discovered Mary was with child. He wanted to believe the best of Mary, but the vision of another will never suffice for doubting hearts.

Accepting what God said, this good, humble carpenter of Nazareth stood ten feet tall with the warmth of his relief. When the angel appeared to Joseph, nobody welcomed the visitation more gladly. To Joseph, the angel did not begin by saying, "Fear not." But it was part of his message: "Fear not to take unto thee Mary thy wife."

All that the angel said to Joseph may not be recorded for us in the Gospel of Matthew, but there is enough to show Joseph's faith. From that moment, the angel never again appeared to Mary. Joseph accepted the responsibility and became her faithful protector. The angel came to Joseph after Jesus' birth to warn that Herod was seeking to destroy the child. Joseph was to take Mary and the baby down to Egypt immediately.

It is significant that the angel came to Joseph rather than to Mary. This itinerant carpenter left his little workshop, taking whatever tools he had, putting Mary and Jesus on a donkey, and slipping away toward Egypt by night. Thus the child was not found by Herod's soldiers. Probably this was the greatest escape we know anything about. God guided Joseph, a faithful and godly man who so readily accepted God's word to him.

No other angel voice ever came to Joseph. It was unnecessary, because Joseph was godly and faithful and reliable and needed no more special guidance. He worked long hours with hands strong and scarred. He had little to offer the Son of God when he became the Son of man—only poverty and hard work. Jesus was reared in the time when sparrows were sold for a farthing, the next smallest coin in value to a mite. It was bargain day when they could get two sparrows for a farthing, or five for two farthings. This was the food of the peasants of Palestine. Sparrows were the only meat they could afford—it was company dinner as well as the daily menu at the house of Joseph.

What a wonderful privilege this godly man received by believing the message of the angel, taking God at his word, and doing the best he could by his work and his family.

Song of Adoration

On these three special occasions, angels brought messages from God to a chosen few: Zacharias, Mary, and Joseph. These messages informed them of the future and told them what to do to obey God. But what about us? Those messages do not apply. There is a message of the angels for us, however, which came on that night when the choirs of heaven bent down and sang the good news to the whole world. Their theme was *adoration*. They sang songs as only angels can sing, of praise and glory to God.

"Glory to God in the highest," the angels sang to the shepherds, "and on earth peace, good will toward men."

The greatest choir earth has ever known sang to a modest congregation, small in number, humble in appearance. If only we could cease apologizing for what we have to offer God and just give what we have in a spirit of love and adoration! Our spirit, our faith, our obedience—what we are on the inside is what counts with God.

The shepherds were modest men, humble men, outdoor men. They were accustomed to noises at night and things that frightened their flocks. They weren't men easily spooked. But when they saw the angel, "The glory of the Lord shone round about them: and they were sore afraid"

(Luke 2:9). Quickly, the angel reassured them: "Fear not!" Dumbfounded and thrilled, they listened as though in a trance.

After the angels departed, the shepherds said, "Let us now go even unto Bethlehem." And they went to adore the newborn child of whom the angels had told them.

Do you know anything about sharing the angels' adoration? Have you come to adore him? In your heart, in childlike wonder, do you commit yourself to him? It doesn't matter how beautiful or expensive or exciting the packages under your tree; if you do not have the gift of Christ in your heart, you can never truly experience Christmas.

A group of soldiers went into a mission school classroom in a foreign land where they had just driven out an enemy force that had held the area in bondage. The children recognized the American uniforms they had been taught to regard as their enemy and they were frightened. The soldiers, wanting to liberate the mission teachers and assure the children of their safety, recognized the fear in the children's eyes. But the soldiers could not speak their language, and the missionaries could not understand English. Searching for a way to communicate their good will, one soldier's mind went back to his childhood, back to Sunday School, back to Sunbeam Band. He started to sing, in English, "Jesus loves me! this I know,/For the Bible tells me so."

The children couldn't understand those words, either, but they recognized the music and knew the words in their own language. They understood the universal message.

What song, what language did the angels sing as they bent near the earth with heaven's doxology? I don't know. But I do know they sang to our hearts as well as to the shepherds' that night: "Unto you is born this day in the city of David a Saviour, which is Christ the Lord."

One songwriter has shown us a wonderful glimpse of songs the angels cannot sing, however:

> But when we sing redemption's story,
>   They will fold their wings,
> For angels never knew the joy
>   That our salvation brings.

7

Seeking Shepherds

(Luke 2:1–14)

Can we say that one night in history, or one story in the Bible, or one event in the affairs of men is greater than all others? If we consider the multiple promises of God, the prophetic passages proven true, and the eternal consequences following, the greatest night of all must be the night when Christ was born.

What about the morning he arose from the dead? Perhaps. But if he had not been born, he could not have died for our sins. If he had not died, he would not have risen from the grave. The night of nights, the crucial event in human history can only be the birth of Jesus in Bethlehem.

Five words stand out in the beloved Christmas story as told by Luke: star, shepherds, song, stable, and Saviour.

The Star

Without a star we do not have the complete Christmas story. Everybody needs a star in his life. The Wise Men followed their star; we must follow ours, for Jesus Christ, in the book of the Revelation, is "the bright and morning star" (22:16). To put on a Christmas pageant, you have to

67

have a star. You need shepherds, and singing, and a stable.
But even if you had all these, without the Saviour you
wouldn't have Christmas.

Because Jesus was born there, the little town of Bethlehem is famous. It is still a very small place, a rather sad
little village—poverty-stricken, not very clean, and with
no industry at all. Yet this was the place that Jesus glorified
by his birth.

Great astrologers from the East came to seek him because they had "seen his star in the east." Thus far he
hadn't spoken a word. Thus far he seemed only another
baby. Thus far he had performed no miracles. Yet, men
came from a great distance to honor him—this newborn
baby who was the King of kings. "Where is he that is born
King of the Jews?" the Wise Men asked, seeking the child
to worship him.

The Shepherds

Outside the city of Bethlehem, there is a certain mountainside called today "the place of the shepherds." It is
thought that it is the spot where the angelic chorus
announced the birth of the Christ child to those who
watched their flocks by night.

If the spirit of Christmas is going to be meaningful to
us today, if the story of Christmas is to remain alive in our
hearts, we must get into the story ourselves. The only place
that we could possibly fit in would be among these lowly
men, these shepherds. They wouldn't mind our being there.
But you and I might not have wanted to crowd into the

stable with them. We would have looked at their garments and considered them uncouth. Shepherds were not the best-paid people in the world—then or now. They were men who spent much time alone. They did not have much education or culture. Yet, to this group came that first angelic announcement—to these people who probably could not read or write, who were not of the privileged, who could not even observe the ceremonies at Bethlehem and Jerusalem. Here in the darkness of night shone the brightest light; the most glorious song the world knows anything about was heard in the stillness of the hillside. We always marvel at the unexpectedness of God.

The shepherds were Jews, however, and they had a dream, a long dream, a dream that stretched from the first chapter of Genesis across the centuries of time—through bad years, good years, dark years, and hard years—a dream of hope. It was built on the promise that one day God would send a deliverer—a Messiah.

One day God's people would throw off the shackles of Rome, they believed. Just as once their ancestors had dreamed of release from Egyptian taskmasters, they looked forward to a day when their Messiah would come.

Their dream began to be fulfilled that night.

God's Thoughtfulness

In the story of the shepherds we discover not only the faithfulness of God, but also the thoughtfulness of God. Probably this was as lowly a group as he could have found together. "I need you," he told those humble people. "I

need you to tell the story; I need you to repeat the glad
tidings; I want you to spread the good news." Life had
been hard for them, but God chose them for a glorious
experience. They must have been transfixed for a moment.

Certainly these shepherds were not expecting the great
God of the universe to come down among them. Have you
expected him to visit you today? That may be the reason
he does not seem to you to be nearby, even at a Christmas
service. Whether you expect him or welcome him or notice
him, he is always there. "Where two or three are gathered
together in my name, there am I in the midst of them,"
Jesus promised (Matt. 18:20).

Often a shepherd would be by himself for weeks at a
time with his sheep. This situation was not quite the usual;
several shepherds seemed to be camping together. To
counteract the quietness of the night and the dreariness of
life (life can be so *daily*), those who kept the night watch
frequently sang; who was listening anyhow? It would quiet
the sheep. Perhaps one of them would whittle a reed, and
that was the only accompaniment they had. It was like the
monotony of the cowboy's watch—in the loneliness, his
guitar quieting the cattle, soothing his own spirit as he
sang to the sky or to himself.

This holy night God came down and gave the shepherds
something to sing about. He announced good news which
we have sung about ever since. The shepherds had many
hard times, many unpleasant reports to make. Often they
had to go into Bethlehem and tell their masters, "We lost
some sheep last week. The winter weather killed some, the

predatory animals took some, and some were stolen. We watched, but in spite of our watching, some of them are gone." They had so many bad reports, only God could have been thoughtful enough to give them a good report to bring into Bethlehem.

It seems that I have delivered so many death messages in my years as a minister that it is a wonderful thrill to have good news to tell. All of us hear enough sad news that it is a joy to listen again to the good news that God sent a Saviour to redeem the world.

To these lonely men God gave the opportunity of telling the "good tidings of great joy, which shall be to all people." Hearing the news, the shepherds made a resolve. "Let us now go even unto Bethlehem," they said. When they went, they were rewarded, finding the Christ child in the manger.

Who Kept the Sheep?

A little girl, listening to her teacher tell the story, asked, "Who kept the sheep while they were gone?" It was a good question. The sheep probably didn't seem very important right then. Epochal events make some things fade into smaller perspective. But any man who gives himself to Jesus will find his business does not suffer. I wish many more men could understand and believe that. Putting God first does not mean that anything else will suffer because of it; but if you don't put him first, everything else will suffer because of it.

The shepherds returned to their routine duties better

workers and better men. They had a wonderful **report to** make and they wanted everybody to share their joy.

The first men who heard about the birth of Jesus couldn't keep it quiet. I wonder what has happened to us. Have we heard it too many times? How can we bear to keep it quiet? It is the only news in the world that will change the destinies of many lives.

These shepherds went about their work rejoicing. I think God would have us rejoice. Christmas should be a season to bring joy to our hearts, a joy that lasts all year long. Do we enjoy our religion as we should? Do we know anything about the deep joyfulness that results from the peace in our hearts "that passeth all understanding"? Do we share it as we should?

The Song

That night the shepherds heard the best song, the most glorious music, that has ever been sung. Handel said that, in his opinion, the announcement was a solo part. But on the refrain, "Glory to God in the highest, and on earth peace, good will toward men," surely all the angelic choir must have sung together.

This choir came from heaven where everybody sings— sings together with nobody off key—everybody knowing the words, everybody knowing the music, and everybody knowing the joy.

Talmadge, an eighteenth-century preacher, used to call this angelic song "The Sky Anthem." That is a beautiful thought, isn't it? God shaped the darkness, lifted up the canopy of the mountainside, and made it into a cathedral. He brought the angels down close to sing and rounded up the shepherds from their watch to listen. The beautiful music that was sung that night has reechoed through the centuries of sin on this earth. Through the ages we hear the lingering strains of "Glory to God in the highest, and on earth peace, good will toward men."

At Christmas, we celebrate the greatest night in the history of the world. Yet we refer to it as "the holiday season"—a time of fun, friendship, and festivity. But before it was a holiday, it was the "holy day" of God. The night when God came down—imagine, God dwelling with us as a baby! That is about all a stable could stand! A member of the Godhead, of the Trinity, who had laid the foundations of the world, became a helpless infant in a little stall, beside the humblest of the animals he had created. No wonder the angels sang!

If the music we sing is not biblical, if what we preach does not tell God's story, then we have no right to expect others to listen. But if our words reflect the Word of God, we ought to join together in singing, "Glory to God in the highest!"

The Saviour

The angels' song would have been empty and futile if the *Saviour* had not been there in the manger in Bethlehem. Finding Mary and Joseph was not the purpose of the shepherds' visit. The Scriptures say that "they found Jesus." If Jesus hadn't been there, they would not have found fulfilment of heart, because God's love was born that night. We learn more about love from this story of how God's Son was born in Bethlehem than we find in any other place.

"What about the cross?" you say. Yes, but we have to go to Bethlehem first.

Many people think with great longing of going home for Christmas. Each of us thinks of home tenderly at this time of year. But if we do not go to Bethlehem for Christmas, we really haven't had a genuine Christmas at all.

We cannot all travel around the world to the actual town in Israel, of course. And if we did, we might be disappointed. One wealthy man said he lost his faith when he saw Bethlehem, because if God would let his Son be born in such a dirty place, he couldn't be much of a God. I think that just goes to show how great he is and how much he loved us. That is how we need to go to Bethlehem, remembering in our hearts and minds how God loved us.

There were people living in Bethlehem that night who God loved. If the shepherds were outside our city, outside our church, would we throw open our doors and welcome them in? There is not a person that we may find to help in our city at Christmas who will not have more than Jesus had when he was born. Not many people live in barns. Not many babies are sleeping in hay these days that we know about—not in our country. Not many newborn children have only swaddling clothes. Not many have nothing at all.

Joseph and Mary, at the end of her days of purification, had to present the child at the Temple and bring a sacrifice. The offerings were a part of their worship, commanded by God when he gave Moses the plan for the tabernacle. If when the Israelites came to the tabernacle to worship they had no gift, the Temple would furnish them one. Everybody had to bring an offering.

When Joseph and Mary came to the Temple with Jesus, they may have had nothing to offer. The lowliest thing one could offer was a pair of turtledoves. They had no ox, no lamb. Jesus himself was the real Lamb—without spot, without blemish, tested by three years in public ministry, —led to the altar of the cross thirty-three years later. He was a son of poverty. His parents went into the Temple with only turtledoves to offer as sacrifice. Jesus became the poorest rich man that ever lived. It is hard to realize how much the Son of God gave up for us. Straw, swaddling clothes, a manger—only the beasts had less. Violence, cursing, taunt of illegitimacy—all of these insults were hurled at Jesus on earth.

Unlimited Joy

Jesus had a cradle, and a cross, and a crown. God gave him the crown. But we gave him the cross. And from the animals, the lower creation, Joseph and Mary borrowed a bed for the baby. When God gave everything for us, are tithes and offerings too much to ask? Sharing around the world, is it too much to ask? Singing the songs of Zion, is this too much to ask? The shepherds left their sheep and went out to tell the good news. Is that too much to ask?

When we stand before an open grave and realize that only in Christ can we hope to see our loved one again, it is not too much to ask. The angels said to the shepherds that "great joy . . . shall be to all people."

In the few countries around the world where I have had the privilege of traveling, I have seen in the little stores various nativity scenes—the Madonna, the shepherds, the Wise Men, the baby Jesus. The face of the baby Jesus was always colored just like the faces of the people who lived there. You can't help noticing it. And they are right: he came to *all* people. They are saying, "He's come down to us. He is *our* Saviour." He is the Saviour of all mankind.

Unrestricted joy! What a great song, what a wonderful message: Hallelujah, what a Saviour!

8
Willing Watchers

(Matthew 2:1–14)

Usually, men are not born kings. They are born princes. After the ruling monarch dies, then they inherit the kingship. But Jesus' birth was unique. The Wise Men were searching, not for just a baby, but for the "King."

"Where is he that is born King of the Jews?" the strangers asked Herod. Here begins the unfolding drama of the double search. Early in the pages of the Old Testament, we find the God of heaven coming down into the Garden of Eden and searching for Adam and Eve, saying, "Where art thou?" They had turned away from God wilfully; the first pair chose to break the perfect fellowship that they had enjoyed with God by disobeying him. Then God began searching for them. At last, he sent his Son to bring mankind back into the divine fellowship.

In the beginning of the New Testament, we find this other question, "Where is he that is born King of the Jews?" When the Lord Jesus Christ came into the world, we have the other act of the drama of the double search. Men began to hunt for God in the way destined to find him: "Where is he that is born King of the Jews?"

Matthew, throughout his Gospel, recognized Jesus as King and set forth his kingship. The Wise Men declared, "We have seen his star in the east and are come to worship him." A new star arose in the East—his star.

The Star Phenomenon

Many explanations have been offered concerning this star, this celestial phenomenon that took place. Some have said that it was the juxtaposition of certain planets. Others have said it was some artificial thing, or a vision. But there is only one acceptable explanation—that it was a miracle of God. God created a sign in the heavens so that men might know of the miracle of Incarnation which had taken place on the earth.

Men can do many things, but only God can hang a star in the sky. These astronomers, though they knew little compared to those in our day, recognized that. There is never any conflict between true science, true knowledge, and the true God. When science has separated from the church, then either the church has gone wrong or science has gone wrong, for perfect knowledge always coincides with the revelation of God.

In the dark world of Palestine under Roman rule, when for nearly four hundred years there had been no word from heaven for God's people, it seemed that the stars were not shining very brightly. Then the Lord God of heaven put up a new star, so that men might have something to guide them through the dark days.

Feeling Your Smallness

Any man can look up at a star and see there the radiance of God. God speaks to each man in his own tongue and according to his own understanding. The Wise Men would not have listened to a sermon. The angels' appearing to them would not have meant as much as it did to the shepherds, for the Old Testament heritage of the Jews prepared them to understand and accept the message of angels. But when there was need for a new message, God hung a star in the sky. It was God's way of saying, "This is my beloved Son. Seek him. Hear him. Serve him."

If men never look up to the heavens, if men do not follow stars, they never get much out of life. Perhaps they are not still enough to look, most of the time. Theodore Roosevelt loved to look at the stars. One night he took some of his friends outside his home to gaze through his telescope. After they had peered into the heavens a while, Roosevelt remarked, "Now we are small enough, let's go in."

That sign, that star in the east, needs to shine brightly into the lives of men today who, in grabbing for riches or for fame, or even in searching for the meaning of life, so often forget the Christ of Christmas. We are prone to lose him in the multitude of things that are mere Christmas wrappings, until all the material glitter of Christmas becomes more important to us than the true gift of Christmas, the Christ child sent from God. Then God says to us, "Look again at my Star. He will make you feel the unimportance of material things."

The Spirit of the Wise Men

We need to develop something of the spirit of the Wise Men who saw his star in the East and formed one great purpose—to find him and worship him. There are many legends concerning the Wise Men, but there are some truths of which we can be certain. In the second chapter of Matthew, these striking figures walk across the pages of the Bible and then out into obscurity again. We do not know their names, we do not know their origins. We only know that because they saw Christ, they went back another way and with a different spirit.

Once a plane was in trouble in the Swiss Alps. Many Americans were aboard, including Bob Hope. The pilot spent some time hunting for a place to land. As is often the case in such emergencies, there was fear and prayer—perhaps in that order. Finally the plane came in to a safe landing. Bob Hope stood up in the quietness and said, "Now, folks, you can go back to the same old life you gave up twenty minutes ago."

But the individual who actually comes to the manger and the cross and the empty tomb, and in reality recognizes that this is Jesus, the Son of God, the King of earth and heaven, that person will never be satisfied to go back to the old life. It never tastes the same, it never feels the same, because you are not the same. You have a new life, a new hope, a new dream, a new consolation, and a new Master—things are never the same. If you slip back into sin and taste it again, you find that the wine mocks, the sin smites, the heart hurts, and it is never the same. The only real peace comes from seeing the radiance of the star and seeking the Christ child.

Where did these Wise Men come from? Maybe from Arabia. Perhaps they came from Persia in the Far East, or from Babylon in the Near East. Legends have given them names. Actually, we do not know their names, except to call them "Wise Men," because of what they did. How many there were, we are not told. Some scholars believe there may have been as many as twelve. Tradition has settled on three, because there were three different kinds of gifts. But it may have been that the men chose three from among them to offer their gifts.

What kind of men were these? They were patient men; they studied the slow-moving stars and scanned the almost unchanging heavens. They were students of the universe, the mightiest creations of God.

Suddenly, in one heart-stopping moment, as they looked up at the heavens, they made a great discovery. They cried aloud in amazement. No longer were the pages of their ancient manuscripts aged and brittle, but alive and contemporary. Their eyes beheld what their predecessors had been looking for through the centuries. They shouted their equivalent of "Eureka!" Suddenly the labors of years seemed nothing. With gladness in their hearts, they recognized the sign of the star.

Searching the Sky

They were not Jews. Perhaps they were pagans to our way of thinking. But they were men searching for the knowledge of God. They studied the sky which he had created. It was open to them, and as the psalmist said, "The heavens declare the glory of God; and the firmament sheweth his handiwork" (19:1). With perseverance these men had waited for the fulfilment of God's promises. Now it was time to act.

How long was their journey? They could scarcely have arrived the same night that Christ was born. Some feel that it was the fortieth day, that they came the day of the Christ child's presentation at the Temple. Others feel that it was the twelfth day, and that this is where the idea of "the twelve days of Christmas" originated. Nevertheless, some days later than the shepherds, the Wise Men came to Bethlehem.

Through weary days and nights they had tracked the star across the featureless desert. If you hitch your life to a star and seek Jesus above all other things, if you have a divine purpose in your life, it will always cause you to give up comfort. Following Jesus always demands sacrifice.

God gave these men definite guidance, for this new star appeared in the East where they were. God always gives special revelation to his people for the need of certain hours. In the darkness of our sorrow, the deepness of our troubles, the multitude of our problems, there is sufficient grace through the sympathetic Saviour. In the halls of the hospital, there is the Great Physician, for Christ said, "I will never leave thee nor forsake thee."

God provided the pillar of fire by night and the pillar of cloud by day to lead the Israelites out of Egypt. God has always asked his people to look up, and when they have looked up to him, he has always guided them. When we go astray, it is usually because we, like Simon Peter, have looked down, and then we begin to sink.

As the Wise Men searched the heavens, the star appeared in the sky. That was all they needed for a while. They started out on the evidence of God's revelation. Some of us want to go down to the end of the street and peep into heaven and see what it is going to be like before we start on the journey. Some of us want all the strength that we shall ever need, right now, lest we fall by the wayside next year. But God gives just enough strength for the day and enough starshine for the night.

The Wise Men neared the end of their journey, and the star was visible no longer. They entered Jerusalem and asked directions to the palace. Surely a king would be born in a palace, they reasoned. Herod was king in Jerusalem (though a vassal of the Romans); therefore Herod would know about this new king that was born.

Logical thinking could not have been more wrong. King Herod was evil and jealous—not even a Jew, having no rightful claim to the throne. As soon as Herod learned the purpose of the Wise Men, he began his own search, but for a different reason. "Where is this child to be born?" Herod asked his scribes anxiously. "Where is this Messiah mentioned?"

The students of the scrolls, the men who knew the laws of Moses, the men whose duty was the preservation of the Word of God, answered Herod, "The Messiah is to be born in Bethlehem," and quoted the prophecy. But they went right back to their dusty libraries, no better than they were before. Some people have a historical knowledge of the Bible; they know Jesus Christ was born in Bethlehem, that he died, that he rose again. If people ask, they can quote the facts, but they have no experience of it for themselves. There is no joy, no urgency, no searching. If Christendom goes on the march in our time, it will have to be led by men who search for a star to follow, like these men who had a goal, a guide, and a purpose.

Symbolic Gifts

The Wise Men brought *symbolic gifts* with them. They had a great quest, and they gave it everything they had.

What do we offer Jesus? Christmas is a time of sharing— a time of getting or a time of giving. It ought to be a time of love. "For God so loved . . . that he gave his only begotten Son," we are told. Because we love, we also must give.

First, the Wise Men gave gold. Gold was a gift fit for a king. It was a symbol of royalty, but it was a very practical gift. Joseph and Mary were poor people. Perhaps this money was used to finance their trip to Egypt. Where do we get the idea that money is dirty, that it ought never be mentioned in the house of God? It is nothing more than a transfer of ourselves, of our devotion, of our dedication.

A young man came one year at the Christmas season, saying he felt the call of God in his life. He had nothing in his pockets, but he said, "I come to give myself; this is all I can give." This is what God gave to us—himself. It is what he wants from us—ourselves. If God's work lacks gold, it is because he does not really have the hearts of the people who claim to belong to him. For if he really had *us,* he would have what we have. Where a man's heart is, there will his money be also. The Wise Men went searching for a king, and their whole hearts and lives were in it.

Next, they brought frankincense, a rare and expensive spice used in worship. This gift was symbolic of the prophetic office of Christ, whose whole life and death were pure and fragrant in the sight of God.

Then there was myrrh, for a king who was also a priest. The priests offered myrrh with the sacrifices, a symbol of suffering, prophetic of the cross. It was a bitter herb that also had medicinal properties and reminds us that Christ was the Great Physician.

Did the Wise Men understand what their gifts meant? I doubt that they did. But these gifts were what they had; these were the products of their countries, and they gave to God what they had available. He does not ask us for what we do not have. He wants us to use what we have to give, in his name, even if it is only a cup of cold water.

A Worship Experience

When the Wise Men came to Bethlehem, they had a *worship experience.* They worshiped the child born King of the Jews. They saw Mary, they noticed Joseph, but they worshiped the baby Jesus. To worship is to pay homage, to prostrate oneself in humility, to magnify another above ourselves.

These visitors were men of wealth and wisdom, but they fell on their faces before the young child and adored him. After that worship experience, they received a new revelation of God's will. They heard the voice of God telling them not to return to Herod but go back another way. They didn't follow a star on their way home, they followed the voice. Sometimes God will give us a sign, sometimes the fleece will be wet, and sometimes we have to follow the instincts of our own hearts. But in the communion with God that follows worship, we will have impressions from God. The voice of God will speak to us.

Herod never saw the star. He was unprepared to worship, and he tried to find Jesus by proxy, and that never works. His request to the Wise Men to bring him news was only a smooth tongue covering up an evil heart.

The men who were looking for the star saw it. And after the Wise Men left Herod's palace, they saw the star again. It stood over the house where the child was, giving them precise guidance.

A star, as we think of it, has five points. This star had five qualities: it was a star of hope, a star of love, a star of peace, a star of joy, and a star of eternal life. These should be the blessings we find in our lives as we follow Christ's star.

Of all people, we who belong to God ought to be the ones to say, "Merry Christmas! Joy to the world!" You and I, of all people, ought to be able to sing the songs of Jesus' nativity, keeping our eyes on the star that rules the universe, for this is the sign of the Lord.

9
Missing the Messiah

(Luke 2:7, 27–34; Matthew 2:1–3)

There is a Christmas story of our day called, "The Man Who Missed Christmas."

George Mason's life was centered in his business. He lived alone, and one Christmas he refused all invitations. His brother's family had urged him to come there, but the children always made so much noise. Besides, he would be expected to bring presents for his nephews and nieces. Instead, he had bought himself some good records and planned to sit alone, listening and enjoying them.

On Christmas Eve, after his employees had left, George Mason went into the office vault to get a little extra cash. Soundlessly, on newly-oiled hinges, the great door swung shut behind him. Sudden darkness and the final click of the automatic lock startled him into panic.

Desperately he pounded on the door. Then he realized no one would hear him. Everyone was gone, even the cleaning women. He began to remember how men had suffocated in vaults.

Surely he could make it overnight, he consoled himself. In the morning his employees would arrive and open the vault. Then he remembered that the next day was not a working day, it was Christmas! His heart pounding with fear, he wondered if he would have enough air to last two days. He calmed himself and tried to think. It was a new vault. Hadn't he heard something about a "safety hole"? Feeling around in the darkness, finally he located it at the top of the back wall—too small for burglars but enough for air.

He sat down on the floor of the vault to wait out the endless hours. Christmas Eve and Christmas Day passed. He was alone, as he had planned. But he was uncomfortable, hungry, and thirsty in darkness so dense he could almost feel it brushing his face.

The day after Christmas the chief cashier arrived and unlocked the vault, but did not open the door. Without anyone seeing him, George Mason staggered out and tottered to the water cooler.

Then he took a taxi to his solitary apartment and freshened up a bit. Back at the office, nobody had missed him. Nobody even asked him how he had spent Christmas.

George Mason truly missed Christmas, because nobody at all missed him. After that experience, he placed a card high on the wall of the vault to remind him. It read, "To love people, to be indispensable somewhere, that is the purpose of life. That is the secret of happiness."

Missing the Christ of Christmas

George Mason's experience was more dramatic than most. But he was not the first man—nor the last—to miss

Christmas. There are many ways in which we may miss Christmas. We may miss it even in the welter of tinsel, trees, and symbols. We may miss it in the songs we sing out of the depths of memory rather than out of the depths of sincere reverence.

We may even miss Christmas at church. Christ said, "God is a Spirit: and they that worship him must worship him in spirit and in truth" (John 4:24). Perhaps everything about the Christmas celebration is so familiar we have lost the wonder of it all. We have lost our spontaneous love in giving; sharing with the poor has become a thing of civic duty. "Silent Night, Holy Night," and "O Little Town of Bethlehem" have lost their thrill; their repetition begins to sound like a broken record. In the hearts of many people they have been replaced by "Rudolph the Red-nosed Reindeer" and "I'm Dreaming of a White Christmas." These miss the Christ of Christmas altogether.

It is understandable that two thousand years ago some of the people around Bethlehem may have missed the first Christmas. How could they have known?

There were some who knew, for God invades history through the hearts of men. Zacharias and Elizabeth, the parents of John the Baptist, knew. Elizabeth said the babe in her womb leaped for joy in the presence of Mary's unborn child.

Joseph and Mary knew. Mary was greatly amazed at the announcement of the angel to her and questioned, "How can these things be?" But she believed and submitted to the will of God. If Joseph had not believed the angel, he would have broken his engagement and put Mary away privately.

Simeon and Anna believed God's promise that the Messiah was coming and they were waiting for him. When they saw the child, they immediately recognized that he was the Son of the Most High.

The Wise Men knew. When they saw the star in the East, they believed that the Messiah of the Jews had come. They knew it had religious significance and they set out on their search to find the newborn King of kings.

If God is to be reached, even today, it will be out of meditation and wonder. Mary treasured her memories of all the great experiences surrounding the birth of her Son and pondered them in her heart.

On that first Christmas, three different kinds of people missed the promised one, the longed-for Messiah, the Son of God. He was missed by secular people, like the innkeeper. He was missed by political leaders like Herod. He was even missed by those supposed to be the most spiritual, the priests in the Temple. We may say that he was missed in the home, the state, and the church. All of these missed the Messiah.

Unwanted by the Secular

First, the innkeeper missed him. The secular world had no place for him. "There was no room for them in the inn" is one of the most haunting sentences in the Christmas story. The Bible doesn't blame the innkeeper. He did not recognize in this poor, tired young couple who asked shelter the great opportunity of his life. With him it was "first come, first served," and "best pay, first place."

Let's make it our town instead of Bethlehem. Let's make this experience contemporary rather than ancient and see how we would react to the situation. Would we want to get involved? Or would we think, impersonally, "Can't this be taken care of by the United Fund?"

The citizens of Bethlehem didn't get together and fight to keep Jesus out. Neither did they vote him out. They just simply crowded him out. It was a matter of preoccupation, a question of priority. Nobody was really moved one way or the other, to spite or to sympathy. When the world loses its touch of tenderness, its warmth of thoughtfulness, its reach of kindness, it will miss Christmas again and again.

The passing of the years had brought great burdens to the Jews, and with the burdens much bitterness. The promises of the prophets had been forgotten. For a thousand years God's people had waited for David's greater Son until in despair they said, "He is not coming!"

Crowded Out?

When Christ came to Bethlehem, it was much like Moses' return to his people in Egypt at God's command. The Bible says, "They hearkened not unto Moses for anguish of spirit, and for cruel bondage" (Ex. 6:9). Moses had come from a mountaintop experience with God, but because of the pressure of their lives they paid him little attention. Because of our calendar of activities, we give priority to many other things rather than to God. We are obligated, we say, to our business, to the secular world; but at church, nobody is checking up on us!

Bibles remain unopened, prayers unsaid, habits of worship are neglected—the flame of faith flickers and nearly goes out. You say you can worship God somewhere else just as well as at church. But tell me, when do you worship God somewhere else? What burdened heart have you prayed for? Where do you put your offerings? How do you let the world know you are a Christian?

Do you really want Jesus in your heart and home this year? I think every child (uncoached by parents) would clap his hands and say, "I want Jesus to go home with me this Christmas." But because of their mothers and fathers, I'm afraid some children will not have Christ in their homes even at Christmas.

The Bible says that at the end of one day of Jesus' ministry, "every man went to his own house"—but Jesus went to the Mount of Olives. "The foxes have holes, and the birds of the air have nests; but the Son of man hath not where to lay his head" (Matt. 8:20). Of course not! The only home Christ wants is in my heart and yours. The only home Jesus could have, the only way he could come in out of the cold, is when he is invited into the hearts of men.

Who wants Jesus? Does the world want him? Did it want him then?

Bethlehem didn't want him. There must have been some

who heard the innkeeper turn Mary and Joseph away. He probably said very little, and on their part was only the clumsy silence of the poor. Embarrassed, I think Joseph and Mary moved on as quickly as they could. There were others in the inn who might have noticed Mary's condition and said, "You can have our room." But the world didn't want to become involved then—and it still doesn't.

Being a Christian means being involved. We are involved in bringing to earth that peace of which the angels sang, spreading God's goodwill among men. We are involved in God's service of love and mercy. We are involved in the message of good news that goes around the earth.

Joseph and Mary returned to Nazareth from Egypt and Jesus grew up there. When he was famous, the townspeople invited him to speak in their synagogue, but he seemed to them to speak strange doctrine and they tried to kill him.

Jesus began his public ministry at Capernaum. There things got so bad that his brothers and his mother (Joseph was probably dead by that time) went over to bring him home lest he be killed. Capernaum didn't want him.

Down in Judea scoffers asked, "Can any good thing come out of Nazareth?"

At the end of his ministry, Jesus wept over the Holy City and God's chosen people. "O Jerusalem, Jerusalem, thou that killest the prophets," he lamented, " . . . how often would I have gathered thy children together, . . . and ye would not!" (Matt. 23:37).

The beloved apostle John wrote, "He came unto his own, and his own received him not. But as many as received him, to them gave he power to become the sons of God" (John 1:11–12).

Unwanted by the State

Herod, the head of the state, didn't want him, either. The political world did not want him around. He pricked their consciences. After the Wise Men did not report back, Herod the Great did not know how to find the child. He was prevented by God from carrying out his evil intentions.

The state was created by God; government was meant to be a theocracy, with God at the head and men as rulers under him. The United States calls itself a democracy—the rule of men. In our time, the trend has been to remove the worship of God from national life. Soon the words "In God We Trust" may even be removed from the coins. In a sense, Christians are guardians of the secular world. Many mount a soapbox and harangue about cold cash and commercialism, but the trouble is that too many Christians go along with it. In the United States 52 percent give lip service to Jesus as Saviour. Therefore we can't isolate society from Christendom. If secular society and government are departing from Christian principles, it is mostly Christians that are responsible—though I trust there is a faithful remnant who still try to go against that tide.

Men are always greedy for more and more power. When

the Wise Men came to Herod with the news that a new king was born, Herod recognized the threat to his throne. "You go find him," he told the Wise Men, "then come back and tell me so that I can go worship him also." He expressed a desire to worship, when he really meant to destroy, as he had killed his own sons to prevent their taking power from him in his old age. Caesar, the man Herod tried to please more than any other, commented that it was better to be Herod's pig than his son. Josephus, the great Jewish historian, said of Herod, "He stole the throne like a fox, ruled liked a tiger, and died like a dog." It was easy for him to think of killing other men's sons—even the Son of God. He had by this time succeeded in murdering everything but his conscience. Suspicion infested his days and terror invaded his nights.

All the rulers of the world who had dealt with the Israelites were haunted by the memory of the survival of the baby Moses. Herod ordered the death of all children in Bethlehem under the age of two, but the infant Jesus escaped, taken to Egypt at the command of God until Herod died. God always has time; rulers of states do not.

Mass murder seems to be characteristic of a godless state, from Herod down to Hitler. When Herod knew that he was approaching death, he ordered that the Jewish leaders whom he had imprisoned be put to death when he died, so that there might be mourning among the Jews. When the state has all authority, and does not acknowledge God, what hope is there for the individual? The dignity of life is lost when there is no room for Christ.

Unwanted in the Temple

But what about the Temple, the church of that day? The *spiritual* leaders did not recognize Jesus, either. They did not know the child brought in by this poor couple from Nazareth was their Messiah, the Anointed One of God.

Only two humble worshipers in the Temple recognized the Christ child when he was brought in by Mary and Joseph. Nothing is said about the priests. The high priest of the time was named in another place, but the priests who failed to recognize the child remain nameless. He who had been promised so long almost departed from God's holy house unrecognized.

God never sounds a bell before him as did many ancient rulers. He speaks in a quiet, inner voice.

Elijah looked for God in the whirlwind, in the thunder and lightning, but after the elements had calmed down, God spoke in a still, small voice. God's voice speaks to the minds and hearts of those who seek him. Had the priests in Jerusalem been "in the spirit on the Lord's Day," like John on Patmos, they would have recognized Jesus as had Simeon and Anna the prophetess.

The Wise Men recognized the meaning of the star because they had been doing their homework. They had been studying their maps and charts with far more attention than the priests of Israel had been giving to their scrolls. If the rulers of Israel had been examining the Old Testament manuscripts, they would have known to expect the Messiah's coming and the Spirit of God would also have moved upon them with conviction.

The tenders of the Temple were so tangled up in their rules, rituals, and regulations that they even outlawed Jesus from the Temple. Many miss the Messiah today just as years ago because they wish to meet him only on their own terms.

The message of the angels was, "Glory to God in the highest, and on earth peace, good will toward men." Do we have goodwill toward strangers and foreigners—men we do not know, those to whom we should take the gospel or send missionaries? Especially, do we have goodwill toward the men we *do* know and wish we didn't?

If he came to our church this year, would he be crowded out by our preoccupation? It has been said that "every life is a mass of incidents; the work of a biographer is in the wisdom of selection." As we go through life, we also have to use wisdom in selection of our interests, our priorities.

A choir from the sky serenaded the earth when Jesus was born, but there was no music in the Temple that day, no rejoicing from an earthly choir. No "All Hail the Power" rang in that house of God because it was spiritually empty. Our hearts and our buildings do not need to be empty and haunted, for any place is a haunted place always if Jesus is not there. Christ promised that "where two or three are gathered together in my name, there am I in the midst of them" (Matt. 18:20).

Will Christ be in your heart, in your church, in your home this Christmas? The Saviour is born: do you have room, will you make room for him?

10

Satisfied Servants

(Luke 2:25–35)

According to the law of Moses, Joseph and Mary brought the baby Jesus to the Temple after he was forty days old "to present him to the Lord" in the prescribed ritual. Perhaps they approached the sacred courts of the Lord with great awe and wonder. At Jesus' birth, shepherds had seen angelic hosts in the fields outside Bethlehem and had come to worship him. If the Wise Men had already come, Joseph and Mary might well have wondered what might happen next. Now they were bringing the infant Son of God into the house of God, where the holy presence had once dwelt. What would God do on this auspicious occasion?

In the century before, the Temple of God had gone through tempestuous times. The pagan Romans had torn down the curtain that divided the Temple courts from the holy of holies. A blasphemous general had stood in the precincts of Jehovah, beat upon his chest and declared himself a god. Then he had committed a crowning sacrilege by offering a pig upon the holy altar. Outraged, the pious Jews of that day begged God to throw a thunderbolt from heaven and strike the intruders dead. But God did nothing. In desperation the faithful prayed, "How long, Lord, how long? How long are you going to endure these things?" They wondered, as perhaps we all have, how long is the patience of God?

This place dedicated to God's honor and glory had been ransacked, violated, blasphemed. The Romans had even used it to stable their horses and cows. It is a strange paradox, isn't it, that the Temple of God was used for a stable, then a stable was used for the birthplace of the Son of God?

Age and Infancy

At first, Mary and Joseph may have felt disappointed that no one took notice of them or of the child. Then an elderly man came up to them, his face aglow. "Then he took him up in his arms, and blessed God" (Luke 2:28). This verse brings to our imaginations one of the most beautiful pictures we shall ever find described in the Scriptures—advanced age with infancy in its arms.

We are not told exactly how old Simeon was, but we are told that the Holy Spirit abode upon him, and the connotation in the original language is that the Spirit was constantly upon this man of God. He was one of those who waited patiently for the consolation of Israel—a term derived from prophecy and referring directly to the promised Messiah. By this phrase those who loved God greeted one another. It expressed their holy expectation that one day the Messiah would appear and deliver them.

Simeon was one of this godly remnant who had not given up hope. He continued to visit the Temple, continued to serve God, continued to pray. At some time there had come to him God's promise of reward for his faithfulness. Before his death, with his own two eyes, Simeon would see the consolation of Israel, would behold the Messiah he longed for, would have final evidence that God indeed would redeem his people. This conviction kept the man faithful and hopeful through long and weary years, perhaps into a very old age. God always holds out blessed promises to his people to encourage their faith in trying times.

We know nothing more of Simeon than this, that he was a devout man who looked for the coming of God's Anointed One. The righteous, faithful few are usually unknown, unnoticed by others, but rewarded by God.

Simeon was not the only one who waited. There was also a prophetess called Anna, a widow at least eighty-four years of age. Waiting had been painful and wearisome for her, also. She had given her life in service to the house of the Lord. Perhaps while Simeon held the child in his arms, Anna came by and was attracted by the joy on Simeon's face and his words of rejoicing. She joined him in praising God.

Wouldn't it be wonderful if we could so easily recognize God when he comes to us unexpectedly, even in the form of a baby? Shepherds, alerted by the angels, found the child in a stable when he was only hours old. The Wise Men came to see the Saviour in a house when he was a few weeks old, perhaps. But the faithful found him in the Temple, which he later called his Father's house. If we want to see the Lord, if we are faithful and expectant, we can always find him in his house.

To fulfil the law of God, Joseph and Mary went to the Temple to offer the required sacrifice and to observe the rites of purification. In the outer courts of the Temple, they had to make some provision for the offering. We are told they offered a pair of turtledoves—the smallest offering that was acceptable. Even then, it may have been a great sacrifice on their part.

Whether or not it became necessary for them to ask the Temple for the turtledoves to make the offering, we cannot be sure. Unless the Wise Men had already brought their gifts, Joseph would have had very little money. It was truly an offering of sacrifice. The Lord's work both then and now is possible only through the gifts of the people. Perhaps the Temple offering—and certainly the flight into Egypt—were financed from the gifts of those who came to worship the newborn Son of God in Bethlehem.

Simeon's Joy

But how did Simeon know? How did he get the revelation? An angel came and told Mary. An angel came and told Joseph. An angel had told Zacharias and the shepherds. But the secret had been well guarded. It had not come to Herod's ears. How did this aged prophet know? "The Holy Ghost was upon him," Luke says (2:25). The

Spirit caught him up in exultation and made him aware
of the fulfilment of the promise.

Simeon immediately broke out into singing for joy that
the time of God's deliverance had come. "Lord, now lettest
thou thy servant depart in peace, according to thy word:
for mine eyes have seen thy salvation, which thou hast
prepared before the face of all people; a light to lighten the
Gentiles, and the glory of thy people, Israel" (vv. 29-32).
A new revelation from God blessed those who were
faithful to the former revelations. It was not just a new
generation; it was a new world, a new opportunity, a
new day, a new hope, a new life.

There are times when we are more sensitive to the Spirit
than at other times. The Spirit of God works in our hearts
and lives when we are ready for him. It may be on a
street corner, or when we knock on a door. It may be that
the silent urge of man's best self prompts him to do something for his fellowman. Simeon recognized the urging of
the Spirit of God, something within. His heart beat faster
when he saw this child. Moved by the spirit of God, he
began to sing.

Who could seal Simeon's lips? When he held the Christ
child, caught up in the vision of God, he felt his heart was
near bursting with a joy only singing could express. Revelation always comes by the Spirit. We today ought also
to seek a more complete revelation of the Christ.

Music is inseparable from Christmas, for Christianity is
really the only singing religion. If you travel to some
parts of the earth, you may find them singing, "Buddha

loves me, this I know," but that is copied from the tune we taught them: "Jesus loves me, this I know." Ours is a spontaneous joy, often too full for mere words. Only music can express what we feel. You take music out of the Christmas season, and what would you have left? No ringing of the bells, no songs of the children, no great music of choirs in the house of God.

Simeon's Expectation

In the Temple, Simeon had been waiting in expectation. This elderly servant of God, when he came into the house of God, usually found it almost empty. I think that grieved his heart, that those who should have been faithful had left desolate the house of God by their absence. Waiting is life's most difficult work. But Simeon never gave up his hope, and because he didn't, God rewarded him. God always rewards those who are faithful. The revelation of God came, expectation was fulfilled.

When Alexander the Great of Greece crossed over into Asia, he gave away all his personal belongings. Those who received what he was parceling out said, "Sir, what will you keep for yourself? You will be on a long campaign and you may need some things. You may come back and need some of these things. What will you keep for yourself?"

"I'll keep hope," Alexander said.

That which we must keep, that which God wants every heart to keep for itself is hope, the hope of the Christ child. How sad were the hearts of the two disciples on the road to Emmaus when they said to the stranger, "We had hoped that this one who came was the Son of God. But he was crucified in Jerusalem. He's dead. We *had* hoped . . ."

As long as man can keep hope alive, as long as we can renew our expectation, as long as we can share our faith, we can go on. Simeon waited with spiritual awareness because he listened to and believed God's promises. In faith we also must wait on the Lord for the fulfilment of his promises to us. It was true that before this holy child fulfilled his mission as the Messiah, there was a cross waiting for him. The cross was waiting from the time he was in the cradle. Beyond the cross, there was a crown waiting for him also, the crown of the King of kings and Lord of lords, the day of complete triumph over all the forces of evil. All this Simeon saw in the child he held in his arms.

Simeon's Blessing

After the maiden mother made the presentation of the child, "Simeon blessed them, and said unto Mary his mother, Behold, this child is set for the fall and rising again of many in Israel; and for a sign which shall be spoken against; (yea, a sword shall pierce through thy own soul also,) that the thoughts of many hearts may be revealed" (Luke 2:34–35).

This was not much of a congratulation to the young mother. Strange things, indeed, had preceded this hour. Mary did not understand all the workings of the Lord; she only accepted humbly what the Holy Spirit said would be possible through her. And when she heard that the sword would pierce her heart, I am sure she felt like shaking her head, remembering the sneers in Nazareth, and saying, "Yes, prophet of God, the sword has dug deep already."

But it was of more than that that Simeon spoke. Another day would come—it is difficult for us to think of it at Christmas time—when the sword that pierced her heart was the death of this Son. For Jesus came to die. Only thirty-three years elapsed between the cradle and the cross. But God declared of that brief life, "This is my beloved Son, in whom I am well pleased."

"I have searched diligently," Pilate said, "and I find no fault in this man."

Surely Joseph and Mary left the Temple that day with hearts made so happy by the fresh sign from God that they scarcely thought of the prophecy of suffering.

God's promise, made centuries before through Isaiah, declared, "Though your sins be as scarlet, they shall be as white as snow; though they be red like crimson, they shall be as wool" (Isa. 1:18). We associate snow with Christmas, because in much of our land it is quite common at this time of year. Snow is one of God's best gifts, and one of the most beautiful.

It seems such a shame to have to mar the purity of the snow to make tracks in it. For a while the whole earth is white. The landscape shows God's new and beautiful touch. But under the snow is mud, which is the stuff we usually walk in and live in. Even the snow should remind us of the hope we have of brightness and purity. It was such a dark day until God gave himself for us in Christ, whose crimson blood has forever changed our sinful grubbiness into the whiteness of snow.

Each year, especially at Christmas, I wish we could receive the Lord afresh and anew. "How can that be?" you say, "I'm already a Christian. Can I be reborn again?" No, that is not possible, any more than when Nicodemus asked the Lord that question concerning a new physical birth.

But the sense of discovery which Simeon felt as he held the baby in the Temple could become fresh and new in the temple of our lives. We could pray that, like Simeon, the Spirit of God would fall fresh on us. With Simeon, we might experience the satisfaction of a faithful servant and the thrilling expectation and fulfilment of God's promises. Then we would be able to say with Simeon, "Lord, now lettest thou thy servant depart in peace, . . . for mine eyes have seen thy salvation."

It is not always death to die. Sometimes I stand by an aged saint and hear repeated the words of Paul, "I have fought a good fight, . . . I have kept the faith: henceforth there is laid up for me a crown of righteousness" (2 Tim. 4:7–8). I thrill with that expectation.

Simeon had grown old in the service of God. This world had no more allure for him. He was ready to go home. All that he wanted was to see Jesus.

If that is our hope, our expectation also, then we are indeed ready to depart in peace.

We praise God anew at Christmas that Jesus has come into our hearts. Hope lives because of him. Faith reigns in our lives because of Jesus. There is peace in the soul because we have really seen Jesus and are satisfied with him. We can agree with Pilate that we, too, have searched Christ's life and found nothing wrong in it.

We can say to God, "He is our Saviour, in whom we are well pleased."

Because of this holy birthday, we understand a little more of how much God loves us. And we thank him for it. This is the time to spread the good news, to publish it everywhere, to sing it and shout it, to say a word about Jesus in everything we do.

"For God so loved the world, that he gave. . . ." That's Christmas!

11
Childhood of Christ

(*Luke 2:40–52*)

The sentimental world, as it celebrates Christmas, loves to think of the child Jesus as an infant in a manger in Bethlehem. A baby is appealing and helpless and lovable. As long as Christ is just a baby, once a year they can celebrate his birthday and then disregard him the rest of the time. What can a helpless, newborn baby have to do with daily life?

But Jesus Christ was not born to remain a baby. Let us allow him to grow; let us look at the childhood of Jesus. The time of his growth into manhood is covered by a curtain of silence. We are given one glimpse of him when he was twelve years old. Then we do not see him again until he appeared at the Jordan asking baptism by John the Baptist. His life in the eighteen years between is unrecorded; we call them the "hidden years" of the Master.

"The most wonderful thing about the hidden years," one has rightfully said, "is that nothing wonderful was written about them." Nevertheless, his growing-up years were not hidden away from life. They encompass many things we would like to know about Jesus. Only one tenth of his life is revealed; about nine tenths of it is quite unknown.

The modern saying is, "Publicity is the lifeblood of success." We have a tendency to feel that unless a person's life has a lot of exposure, unless his public relations are well planned and his publicity well timed, his career can never get off the ground. But the truth of the matter is that much of the greatness in any life is prepared in unknown and silent years. Jesus lived about thirty hidden years before he began his ministry.

A Refugee Child

Jesus was a refugee child. He was taken from the city of his conception before his birth because his mother and Joseph had to go from Nazareth to Bethlehem for the taxation. Then he had to be carried away quickly into Egypt because of Herod. "Out of Egypt have I called my son" (Matt. 2:15; cf. Hos. 11:1) was the word of prophecy. After the death of Herod the Great, Joseph and Mary returned with Jesus to Nazareth, where he grew to manhood.

A little town is a good university in which to study human nature. In Nazareth, there were many kinds of local people; Romans, Phoenicians, and many other nationalities besides Jews lived there. That Jesus studied people carefully is obvious in his preaching.

Nazareth was a despised town, with a reputation all its own. But it was not an isolated place, not a remote area untouched by the world. The child Jesus heard the *tramp, tramp* of Roman legions marching through. He knew what it was to hear the command of a Roman soldier: "Hey, boy, carry my pack," as it was thrown into the lap of a Jewish lad. He was acquainted with the mainstream of commerce that thronged the crossroads of Nazareth.

In the last century, "Go west, young man, go west," was a piece of wise advice given to young men who sought success. But in the days of Josephus there was another saying: "If you want wealth, go north. If you want wisdom, go south." Nazareth—in fact, all of Palestine—was considered "south" from the centers of culture in Greece and Rome.

Jesus did not grow up in an untouched dream world; Nazareth was a rough neighborhood. Yet the surrounding countryside had many quiet places in which Jesus could study nature and could be alone with his Heavenly Father to commune with him.

God had directed the steps of his Son through the foster-father, Joseph, to fulfil the prophecy that the coming deliverer of Israel should be called a Nazarene.

Most of all, we would wish to know more about Jesus' home. What kind of home did he live in?

Jesus' Home

The words of Jesus show he knew what took place in family life. In his parables he spoke often of the children playing in the marketplace. He knew about hungry children begging bread: "If his son ask bread, will he give him a stone?" (Matt. 7:9). Jesus understood the plight of widowhood, for when he went to the Temple he remarked on the widow who gave all that she had (Mark 12:44). Jesus always had a word of kindness for those who bore the problems, the heaviness, the toils of life.

"Suffer little children, and forbid them not, to come unto me: for of such is the kingdom of heaven" (Matt. 19:14). Jesus understood that even the children knew something of the hardships of life. Again and again he said, as did Paul, "Children, obey your parents in the Lord: for this is right" (Eph. 6:1).

Jesus was never ashamed of his home and heritage, and the sacrifices his parents made. Such ungratefulness is not Christian. For everything good that comes into our lives we can turn our minds back in tender memories to all the things that have been done for us, treasuring the little bits of advice, the sacred moments, the pat of the hand, the placing of a strong arm on the shoulder. Jesus recognized these valid human relationships.

Jesus knew what it was to have a humble home. Probably there is not a home anywhere in our community that is more poverty-stricken than was Jesus' home. A one-room house, it had no beds, only sleeping pads they simply rolled out at night. People slept in the garments they wore and rolled their cloaks around them for covers. Usually, there were no fires inside the houses.

The father or eldest son would lead in thanksgiving before and after each meal—probably not more than two meals a day. What did they have to thank God for? Often there was little rice for the bowl, little flour for the bread, little oil for the lamps. Their lives would be considered destitute by our standards today.

Many people never owned a change of garments; they possessed only what they had on, ragged though it might be. If we have worn hand-me-downs, we remember how we longed for something new of our own. Most of these people never even hoped for that. They knew they would never have anything they could call their own except misery, burdens, and sin.

Jesus' Heritage

What heritage did Jesus have in the midst of this poverty? God's Word reaches into the silent years of Jesus' youth and gives us only one glimpse. We see the child Jesus at twelve years of age, with his family, going down to Jerusalem, the Holy City.

Two or three times in his life a Jewish lad was required to go to the Temple. He was taken for presentation on the fortieth day, especially if he was a firstborn male (Ex. 13:12), and a sacrifice was offered after the mother's days of purification (Luke 2:22-25).

When a Jewish boy was about twelve years of age, he would go to the Temple to become officially "a son of the law." It was a thrilling ceremony to participate in, the first time a boy went with his father to worship God.

When Jesus was twelve, he went with his family to Jerusalem. Probably a whole group of relatives made the journey together. Approaching the Holy City, they could see the gleaming dome of the Temple. Surely the boy Jesus felt an awesome, sacred joy in his heart as he arrived at his maturity as "a son of the law." It is quite likely that he had received religious instruction by the local teachers of the law. All his life he had been memorizing the Scriptures as required. "Thou shalt teach them [these words] diligently unto thy children," Jewish parents had been commanded (Deut. 6:7).

The men and boys usually walked together. The women came more slowly behind, bringing the necessary camping equipment. Often more than 500,000 extra Jews came to Jerusalem for the festivals. There were no inns to take care of them. Some, of course, had relatives who would crowd them into their homes. The family from Nazareth would have had no shekels to pay if there had been hotels.

Jesus talked about five sparrows for two farthings; this was the kind of marketing he knew about. The cheapest thing that was offered—this was their daily fare. The Bible says that the common people heard him gladly. Of course! He was one of them. "The Spirit of the Lord is upon me," Jesus said, "because he hath anointed me to preach the gospel to the poor" (Luke 4:18).

At the Temple

As Jesus went into the Temple, he was anxious to see all the ceremonies. First, there was the offering of sacrifices. Then the Sanhedrin, the teachers of the Law, rather than holding their deliberations in private, this one day a year came outside and held their meeting in public. It was not out in the public court amid the noise of the outside world, the bleating of animals, and the clanking of the money changers, but in the Temple forum—the public auditorium, so to speak. All who desired could sit and listen to them. So Jesus did.

He was so fascinated that when his relatives had paid their respects, done their duty, and left, the lad didn't go with them. He did not intend to disobey, probably, but he was completely absorbed. His whole mind was given to this house of God, his true world. This was his realm; they were discussing his Father's affairs. The fact that day and night passed meant nothing to him. His calendar was eternity.

In the meantime, Mary and Joseph started back to Nazareth, their groups traveling in different companies. It was some time before they noticed Jesus was missing. They passed a fearful night and hurried back to Jerusalem.

The strange thing was that Jesus was in the Temple all the time. Because Jesus knew all things, some think that he was picking the teachers to pieces, asking brash questions. Not at all! He was in his realm in God's house, at worship. He was behaving in a reverent manner, drinking in their words and asking honest questions. The Bible says that the teachers of the Law were amazed at the depth of his understanding. He wasn't trying to trick them; he wasn't telling them; he was listening attentively. They were amazed at a twelve-year-old's being so interested. Why wasn't he playing with the other boys?

This was an hour he had waited for. There must have

been times when he asked Mary questions she could not answer. Probably she replied, "Son, when you go to the Temple you can ask the priests. The scribes will be able to tell you." Now Jesus was making up for lost time. This was a great moment in his life.

When his mother and Joseph came, his absorption was broken.

"Don't you know we have worried about you?" his mother demanded.

"Don't you understand," he replied, in effect, "that this is what is important to me? I must be about my Father's business." This was the first of a series of "musts" in the Master's life.

Jesus' Habits

We know something about the habits of Jesus' life. There are not many things we can deduce about his early life, but we know that on the sabbath he always went to the Lord's house, for the Bible says, "as his custom was" (Luke 4:16). Several things we can be sure were the habits of his life.

First, he was a prayerful lad. He learned the prayers of children. He learned from the rabbis; he learned from his mother; he learned from hearing Joseph pray.

Jesus knew his Bible—the Old Testament Law—and quoted it often. His habits in early life showed his sense of mission, even at the young age of twelve.

Jesus was a thinker. It is wrong to take for granted that a man who works with his hands never thinks. What he is doing may have become so mechanical and his fingers may have grown so methodically skilful that his mind is able to turn to other things.

One of the best Bible teachers I ever knew was an unlettered man, a man who had no formal training. There was no church in his community; services were held in the schoolhouse on Sunday mornings twice a month. But Sunday evenings this man would sit down with his family and the Word of God. They would read it together and go over the Sunday School lesson for the next Lord's day. All week long, as this man worked, he would turn that lesson over in his mind and ask God to prepare his heart with wisdom. He was a thinking and a praying man, and he had great influence for God.

Jesus was blessed with a heritage of godliness and hard work in his home. Work became the habit of his life. The Bible says, "Jesus increased in wisdom and stature, and in favour with God and man" (Luke 2:52). The only perfect person who ever lived in all the world was Jesus Christ. He is our pattern. He was a normal boy—but more. He was God's perfect pattern, a volume in one sentence.

He increased in wisdom; that is our mental pattern.

He increased in stature—he grew up. The Bible seems to tell us here that he had a strong body and that he took care of the physical endowments God gave him. He did not indulge in things he knew would bring weakness to his body.

He gained favor—first of all with God, in his spiritual growth. Then also with other people. Man was not made to live alone; a child is a social being. It is up to us as parents to train them, not only at home, but in the community. How else can they learn to live in the world? It is largely up to the home to provide the right pattern.

Why did God give us just one picture of Jesus out of eighteen years of his life? I don't know. But I do know that one picture shows Jesus at church.

That is probably the pattern God wants every parent to remember to help them train their children. And if the children remember only one thing about Jesus as a child, they should remember what happened at the Temple, where he sought to understand more of his Father's business.

12
The Steadfast Star

(Matthew 2:1–10; Revelation 22:16)

When we think of the Christmas star, is it just for a few days while the tree is up? Or is it something meaning-ful and lasting in our lives until Jesus comes? There is really no end to the Christmas season, for the first advent will never be complete until the second advent. The stead-fast star which rose in the East almost two thousand years ago has not yet reached its maximum brightness.

John Jeter Hurt, an outstanding Baptist educator in Georgia whose son is now editor of *The Baptist Standard* in Texas, tells a story from his father's early days.

Mr. Hurt had sold a mule, and he asked one of the men on his farm to take the mule to the new owner in a distant town. The hired man could not read or write, so Mr. Hurt drew a detailed map, marking every crossroad.

"I'm not sure," the man said, puzzled, shaking his head.

"I promised the man I'd have the mule there in the morning," Mr. Hurt said. "It will be cooler if you travel at night. But if you can't read the map, how can you find your way there?"

"Pick me out a star, boss," the laborer replied, "and I'll

have your mule there by morning." No man is ignorant who can seek direction from the stars.

The ancient men of the sea had a saying: "All I ask is a tall ship and a star to steer her by."

When God wanted the attention of the watchful, he hung a new star in the sky beyond all the stars with which men were familiar. The Wise Men, who attached significance to the star, were among the first to hail the Christ child as King.

A Star for All

God's revelations are always fitting and timely. To the Jews who loved wisdom he gave prophecy; to the simple shepherds he gave bright angels; to the wise astrologers he gave the illumination of a new star. Some peoples of the East had a religious cult that depended upon the stars for guidance; therefore God forbade his people to worship the stars (Deut. 4:19). Many pagans felt that gods dwelt in the stars. Satan the deceiver has always tried to get men to worship the creation rather than the Creator.

The coming of the Wise Men is a beautiful part of the Christmas story, indicating that all men could adore the Son of God: the simple and the smart, the rich and the poor, the peasant and the king, both men and angels.

The Christmas star shone for more than a night. Contrary to many of our pageants, the Wise Men did not come the night of Jesus' birth. We do not know what distance the Wise Men traveled—perhaps from Babylon, or even farther. They must have ridden camels, which are not very speedy beasts. Their journey must have taken them several weeks, or even months. That star is a symbol that lingers.

There is a tendency that in self-sufficiency we might lose sight of the star. As the Wise Men approached Jerusalem, they reasoned, "If anybody knows about the child, it will be the king." They forgot that all the wisdom of this world is not necessarily in a king's mind, or in a king's palace. There is wisdom given of God to the people whom he chooses.

Naaman, the Syrian soldier who was a leper, made this same mistake. When he came to Israel seeking a man of God to cure his leprosy, he went to the king. There are times when we rely on our own knowledge and lose sight of the star. The illumination of the star of God is always available, but we don't always look for it.

God has given men signs in many different ways. To the Israelites in the wilderness he gave a pillar of fire by night and a pillar of cloud by day. To the Wise Men he gave a star. "I will not leave you comfortless," Jesus said to his disciples (John 14:18). "I will pray the Father, and he shall give you another Comforter, that he may abide with you for ever" (v. 16).

We do not lose sight of the star when we walk with Jesus; we only lose sight of it when we begin to seek guidance in other places. What does this steadfast star say to us?

Star of Heaven

Jesus Christ is the *star of heaven*, "God with us," the evidence of heaven come down to man. "The Incarnation," one man has wisely said, "is God taking short steps so that men might keep up with him." Stripped of his eternal glory, forsaking the wonderful streets of gold for a stable among men, wrapped in the swaddling clothes of a peasant baby, God's Son was given.

Now that the other gifts are out from under the Christmas tree you may notice that by habit you placed either an angel or a star on the top. Gifts given and packages unwrapped, it may be an appropriate time for us to remember that God wrapped a heavenly gift and gave it to the earth. "For God so loved the world, that he gave his only begotten Son, that whosoever believeth in him should not perish, but have everlasting life" (John 3:16).

This star of heaven was promised many times in the Old Testament. In the first chapter of Genesis we are told that "God said, Let there be lights in the firmament of the heaven. . . . to give light upon the earth: . . . He made the stars also" (1:14–16).

Baalam was a foreign prophet who, though not the most reliable prophet, had great respect for the Israelites because they were God's people. "I shall see him, but not now," Baalam said. "I shall behold him, but not nigh: there shall come a Star out of Jacob, and a Sceptre shall rise out of Israel" (Num. 24:17). An English preacher of long ago wrote about Baalam, "He was not very good, yet a true prophet in this, and his prophecy true, for such is recorded in the book of Moses."

Isaiah wrote, "The Lord shall arise upon thee, and his glory shall be seen upon thee. And the Gentiles shall come

to thy light, and kings to the brightness of thy rising"
(60:2–3).

You have heard often, particularly around a hospital,
"Oh, if it would just be daylight. If the morning would only
come!" Peter knew the darkness of human depravity. He
had only to remember his own denials of the Lord before
the crowing of the cock. He also knew that only one thing
could lift the darkness and make the wounded heart rejoice. He declared, "We have also a more sure word of
prophecy; . . . a light that shineth in a dark place, until
the day dawn, and the day star arise in your hearts"
(2 Peter 1:19).

When our redeeming Saviour was born, there was great
rejoicing on earth. Truly, heaven comes down and glory
fills our souls when the star of heaven rises in our hearts.

Remember that the star at the top of your Christmas
tree isn't just tinsel, but a testimony to God's love.

Star of Hope

Jesus was also the *star of hope*. The Wise Men began
their long and perilous journey on the basis of hope. "We
have seen his star in the east," they said, "and are come to
worship him." The apostle Paul stressed the need for hope
in Christ both here and hereafter: "If in this life only we
have hope in Christ, we are of all men most miserable"
(1 Cor. 15:19).

A few years ago, one of our newest submarines went
down off the continental shelf in the Atlantic. The best
ingenuity of our scientists and engineers had gone into that

ship and it was hailed as a great stride forward in the defense of America. But something happened, and it sank in deep waters. The resources of this giant nation were rushed to the scene, and every possible attempt made to get the men out. But nothing could save them. The last message in Morse code tapped against that metal sunken tomb was, "Is there any hope?" It was repeated more faintly as the oxygen failed and the hand became weaker, "Is there any hope?"

At some time or another, that seems to be the question of every man: "Is there any hope?" An editorial in a recent magazine said, "We are all prisoners of hope . . . and hope is perhaps the chief happiness this world affords."

There is no secure hope for a nation in wealth or brain-power or military might. There is no secure hope for the individual in material things or social position. The only hope of the world is in the star God hung out that night, the promise that Golgotha and the empty tomb would be.

When Jesus was born, God's people had endured four hundred years of darkness; Israel had been through captivity and much suffering because they had disobeyed God and ignored and persecuted his prophets. Most of the Jews fretted about the Roman conquerors but had little faith in God's promise of a Redeemer. Only a few even bothered to say, "Is there any hope?"

Today we hear the cry, "Will there ever be peace again? Is there any hope?" It is the cry of young women for their husbands and the silent tears of parents for their sons. Sometimes it seems that the stars have gone down.

Dr. Charles A. Beard, a great American historian, has summed up the teachings of history in four proverbs, one of which is, "When it gets darkest you may see the stars."

If you are discouraged in your upward journey to the city of God, don't lose sight of the star of hope. "God is light, and in him is no darkness at all" (1 John 1:5). The Lord Jesus is our source of light, and we cannot shine any brighter than his reflection.

Together, the stars give sufficient light at night for men to travel by. The star of Bethlehem became brighter on Golgotha's hill. Though the sky darkened over the reality of the cross, the steadfast star shone ever more brightly out of the empty tomb. It will never set! Its light has always been sufficient for men to find their way through dark dungeons and open graves.

Christ is the one star that can guide through the blackest night. His first rising will be completely fulfilled in his second appearance, yet to come. "Looking for that blessed hope," a New Testament preacher encouraged us, "and the glorious appearing of the great God and our Saviour, Jesus Christ" (Titus 2:13).

The Star Himself

Jesus Christ is the *star himself*. The Creator of the first chapter of the Bible is the star of the last: "I Jesus . . . am the root and the offspring of David, and the bright and morning star" (Rev. 22:16).

The promises of God have been many, but they all are gathered together in Jesus. Those of you who have watched the stars know that the morning star is the brightest gem of daybreak. It is the last star of night to fade, the one which announces that there is a new day approaching on earth.

Jesus Christ is that bright and morning star who came into a world of darkness and announced a new day on earth. Now men can see God. Men who seek God can find him through Jesus. Men can have God's guidance through the Holy Spirit.

We hear so much about "status symbols" these days. We Christians have a status symbol, a star of our own. Jesus promised us, "He that overcometh . . . I will give him the morning star" (Rev. 2:26–28).

An artist, one of the best of the old masters, left all of his paintings unsigned because, he said, "Men may be able to forge my name, but they cannot copy my pictures." And he was right.

The Master of heaven and earth, the Lord of life and death, the star of Bethlehem and Calvary, asks us not only to take his name and be called Christians, but to copy his life, his work, his nature. We are to walk in his name, in his strength, in his light. We are to reflect his light into this world as the moon reflects the sun, so that the world may be illumined by the light of God.

Lloyd Douglas went to visit his old violin teacher one day and found the day had been difficult. Aspiring youngsters had missed the notes and played off-key, scratchily. The visitor could see that the old teacher was discouraged and frustrated.

"What's the good news?" Douglas asked in his characteristic way.

The teacher picked up a padded hammer and struck the tuning fork. "That's the good news," he said. "That's A. It was A yesterday, it is A today, it will be A tomorrow. Regardless of how many people sing or play off-key, it is always A. That's the good news!"

The good news of the Christian it that "Jesus Christ [is] the same yesterday, and today, and for ever" (Heb. 13:8).

He who was the Prince of peace announced by the angels in Bethlehem's field is still the Prince of peace in the midst of international tensions, nuclear bombs, and space capsules. "I am Alpha and Omega," he said, "the beginning and the end, the first and the last" (Rev. 22:13). He is our *steadfast star,* now and forever.

Other BROADMAN BOOKS

By R. Earl Allen

●●●●●●●●●●●●●●

Strength from Shadows

Christian Comfort

Memorial Messages